D1882789

A CRITICAL STUDY OF TRENDS IN E-BANKING WITH SPECIAL REFERENCES TO SELECTED PUBLIC AND PRIVATE SECTOR BANKS

COD | TOTAL ITEMS 1

EKART CN08_E

SDLC1043211001

ELASTICRUNG OHANAODH_RO H --F

PKD: 2025-01-27 10:22:06

DELIVERY ADDRESS

Rajesh
Dr Jagdish Prasad Sharma, Huckam Chand Mandi, near Brhamkumari aasharam, Gudha Road, Gohana, Sonipat Haryana 131301

CITY/STATE Gohana , Haryana

PIN 131301

SUBORDER CODE	QUANTITY
62537848703 | 1111024969846	1

SELLER ADDRESS
GYAN BOOKS PVT LTD.
GYAN BOOKS PVT LTD GYAN AVENUE 12 PRAGATI MARKET ASHOK VIHAR, PHASE2, NEAR AATTAM HOSPITAL NEW DELHI - 110052

SELLER GSTIN:
07AAACG4699N1ZY

Snapdeal Reference No

SLP4426121141

Snapdeal DOES NOT have any Prize Scheme/ lottery / lucky draws.

Need Help? Please visit the 'Profile --> My Orders' section in the Snapdeal App for assistance.

TAX INVOICE (ORIGINAL FOR RECIPIENT)

INVOICE NUMBER : S6B5CB/24/3790
INVOICE DATE : 27-JAN-2025
ORDER DATE : 26-JAN-2025

TOTAL ITEMS 1

SELLER
GYAN BOOKS PVT LTD.
GYAN BOOKS PVT LTD GYAN AVENUE 12 PRAGATI MARKET
ASHOK VIHAR, PHASE2,
NEAR AATTAM HOSPITAL
CITY NEW DELHI / **STATE** DELHI (07)
PIN 110052
GSTIN : 07AAACG4699N1ZY

BUYER
RAJESH
DR JAGDISH PRASAD SHARMA, HUCKAM CHAND MANDI, NEAR BRHAMKUMARI AASHARAM, GUDHA ROAD, GOHANA, SONIPAT HARYANA 131301
CITY GOHANA / **PLACE OF SUPPLY (POS)** - (06) - HARYANA
PIN 131301

ITEM DESCRIPTION	QTY	RATE	TOTAL	DISC	TAXABLE VALUE	IGST	CESS
A CRITICAL STUDY OF TRENDS IN EBANKING WITH SPECIAL REFERENCES TO SELECTED PUBLIC AND PRIVATE SECTOR BANKS SKU CODE: 1111024969846 ORDER NO.: 55073923728 SUBORDER NO.: 62537848703 HSN: 49011010	1	802.0	802.0	146	656.0	0 (0.00 %)	0 (0.00 %)
TOTAL(INCLUSIVE OF TAXES)							Rs. 656

AMOUNT IN WORDS : INDIAN RUPEES SIX HUNDRED FIFTY SIX ONLY
whether the tax is payable on reverse charge basis : NO

Beware of fake Calls/SMS/Emails offering any cash/prize under any fraud scheme/lottery/lucky draw. Do not share any information or pay any amount

DECLARATION
We declare that this invoice shows actual price of the goods described inclusive of taxes and that all particulars are true and correct.

CUSTOMER ACKNOWLEDGEMENT
I RAJESH hereby confirm that the above said product/s are being purchased for my internal / personal consumption and not for re-sale.

For GYAN BOOKS PVT LTD.

Authorised Signatory

©Author

All rights reserved. No part of this work may be reproduced, stored, adapted, or transmitted in any form or by any means, electronic, mechanical, photocopying, micro-filming recording or otherwise, or translated in any language, without the prior written permission of the copyright owner and the publisher. The book is sold subject to the condition that it shall not, by way of trade or otherwise, be lent, resold, hired out, or otherwise circulated without the prior publisher's written consent in any form of binding or cover other than that in which it is published.

The views and opinions expressed in this book are author(s) own and the facts reported by them have been verified to the extent possible, and the publishers are not in any way liable for the same.

ISBN: 978-93-5324-645-7

First Published, 2022

Published by

Kalpaz Publications
C-30, Satyawati Nagar,
Delhi – 110052
Ph.: 011-47034999, 9811692060
www.kalpazpublications.com
E-mail: kalpaz@hotmail.com

Printed at: Gyan Press, Delhi.

Dedicated
to my
Loving Parents

Contents

Acknowledgement

This book is first and foremost dedicated to The Almighty God. His power and guidance have been instrumental in forming the seeds of ideas that have sprung to life in published form.

I Solemn acknowledgement is due to my supervisor Prof. Satish Munjal, Department of Economic Administration and Financial Management, University of Rajasthan without whose guidance and advice this book would not have appeared in the present form. It is indeed my privilege to express gratitude and reverence to him for the keen interest he has taken in the work.

I express my sincere thanks to respected parents and a deep sense of gratitude to my brother and Bhabhi Mr. Ravi Angi, Mrs. Vinita Angi, Mr. Mohit Angi, Mrs. Bhanuja Angi who have been a constant source of encouragement and support which helped me a lot in the completion of this book.

Finally, thanks to my family for having patience with me and allowing me to take yet another challenge that somewhere decreased the amount of time I spent with them. Specially Veronica, my daughter who has made a big part of that sacrifice.

Dr. Sakshi Angi

Preface

It revolution has converted the world into a global village. The thinking structure, work-culture and functioning styles are changing on hour basis. IT has created tremendous job opportunities for the people around the globe as well made the organisations efficient and productive. There has been an IT revolution in the world in the last 40 years. This revolution has altered the way we work and think. It has touched every enterprise, sector, society and government where banking is the most triggered area. In the most of the developed countries like USA, it has been contributed to half of the productive growth and a third of the economic growth over the last five years. In India most of the organisations have already deployed IT to transform their process. Government of India is even practicing e-governance and offering single window solutions to the customers. Recent developments in IT have introduced a plethora of opportunities for development in banking industry too. IT as an enabler has broken all bounds of cost, distance and time. In the pre-1991 era, Indian banking system was suffering from number of internal and external factors, the financial and qualitative aspect was deteriorated but in the post-second banking sector reforms era gained momentum. IT Act of 1999 further accelerated the strength of the Indian banking system, but unfortunately, the biggest sector in the Indian banking sector i.e. public sector banks have not gained as much as private sector. The gap is continuously increasing between the public sector banks and private sector banks and moreover, public sector banks are facing number of challenges regarding the use of e-delivery channels.

Except some banks, others are unable to face the global challenges due to lack of use of advanced technology. The present study investigates the perceptions of e-banking customers and employees and based on these perceptions, some suggestions are made for the survival of public sector banks and will provide an opportunity to the academicians, IT consultants, research scholars, practitioners and students to go through for further detailed studies in this area. Modern technology has transformed the functioning of business. It has bridged the gaps in terms of the reach and the coverage of system and enabled better decision-making based on the latest and accurate information, reduced cost and overall improvement in efficiency. In the Indian context, the financial sector, especially the banking sector has been a major beneficiary from the inroads made by IT. Many new processes, products and services offered by banks and other financial intermediaries are now IT centered. Nowadays many banks are providing the services through e-channels like ATMs, I-banking, M-banking, Tele-banking, Debit cards, Credit cards, etc. Most of the initiatives regarding e-channels are aimed at providing better and more efficient customer service by offering multiple options to the customers.

Keywords Used

ALPM: Stand alone personal computers which were used for a very limited purpose of recording ledger transactions and either had no storage disk or had a very limited storage capacity.

Batch Mode Processing: Processing of transactions on computers after the transactions at the end of the working day in one lot and not as and when undertaken. Also known as offline Processing.

Online Processing: Computerised Processing of transactions and updation of master records as soon as the transactions are undertaken.

Real Time Systems: Computer systems which process the transaction as in online processing and also initiate further action like cash dispensing and balance updation as soon as transaction is done without any manual intervention. (eg. ATMs)

ACH: Computerised clearing of transactions of different banks wherein the participating banks transfer their transactions with other participating banks electronically over a network computer.

RTGS: Real Time Gross Settlement Systems in which the transactions are communicated electronically over a network to the bank which maintains accounts and instantaneously updates the balances.

DVP: Delivery Versus Payment system in which the transfer of securities like Government bonds is accompanied by transfer of cash from buyer of the security to the seller of the security.

Netting: A system of settlement in which transactions among contracting banks are netted out with each other and only final amount either net payment or net receipt is settled through clearing house.

Smart Cards: Magnetic cards which are charged or magnetised for a fixed amount and can be used to transact like currency by transfer of this magnetic charge to the contracting party.

Customer Information Service: It's a computer-based information system about bank's customer which can indicate his savings and spending pattern, his economic activities, etc., which can be useful to the bank.

Microbanking: Banking practice in which the bank's services are based on customers needs as observed by the customer information service.

Distributed Data Processing: The computer processing where in data is stored at different places on different computers but accessed using computer network.

EFT: Electronic Fund Transfer in which the funds are transferred by exchanging telecommunication messages over a computer network.

Financial Telecommunication: Telecommunication of messages relating to financial transactions like funds transfer, payment or receipt of funds confirmation of transactions accounting statements, etc.

Electronic Data Interchange: Transfer of data electronically over a computer network for various purposes like business, financial, transport, travel or administrative service.

MICR Cheque: The Magnetic Ink Character Recognition Cheque is a cheque on which essential items required for the clearing house are recorded in magnetic ink which can be read by magnetic readers and converted into computer data.

Credit Clearing: A clearing service in which bulk payments like dividend or interest payment are made by corporates to their shareholders/depositors by giving details of bank account numbers, amounts etc. directly without any payment instruments like cheques.

Debit Clearing: A clearing service in which the routine pre-authorised payments by the customers are collected by the banks through clearing mechanism without any instrument like cheque.

Network Banking: Banking service organised using computer networks.

Reengineering of Work Processes: Reorganisation of the functions and working of the organisation in light of new technology adopted by the organisation.

Outsourcing: Practice of developing application software for the organisation by involving professional software developers.

Inhouse Development: Practice of developing application software by training personnels within the organisation to develop computer software.

Financial Derivatives: Financial instruments which are not in the nature of business transactions in themselves but are aimed at reducing the uncertainty in the financial transactions by transferring risk for consideration.

Payment System: The payment system means the mechanism of payment like clearing house, Funds transfer, debit/credit clearing, DVP, netting etc.

Total Branch Computerisation (TBC): Policy of computerisation of working in banks wherein all the transactions carried out in branch of a bank are computerised and the branch acts as a independent service provider.

Chapter - I

Introduction

In the present era of revolution in information technology, the economic setup of every country has witnessed tremendous changes in their respective working. The banking sector too has not remained untouched and unaffected by these changes. It has introduced several new processes, as E- banking and innovated its day-to-day functioning.

Today's banking is virtual or innovative banking which denotes the provision of banking and other related services through the extensive use of Information Technology (IT), without direct resource to the bank by customers. The salient features of Innovative Banking are overwhelming reliance on IT and the absence of physical bank branches to deliver banking services to the customers.

E-Banking

E-Banking refers to performing basic banking transactions by customers round the clock globally through Electronic Media. In other words, E-Banking is the application of IT infrastructure with latest equipment and solutions and integrated networks essentially to facilitate smooth and efficient payment and settlement, improved customer service and the resultant increase in profitability.

Modern banking is more information based, speedy and boundary less due to the impact of Electronic Revolution. Modern banks have to be well-versed in Information Technology – its uses and applications. Banking divisions have to be IT based, with the spread of digital technology. E-banking is more of a science than an art.

E-banking is knowledge based and mostly scientific in using electronic devices of the computer revolution. When most business and commerce enterprises tend to become internet working organisations, banking has to be E-banking in the new century.

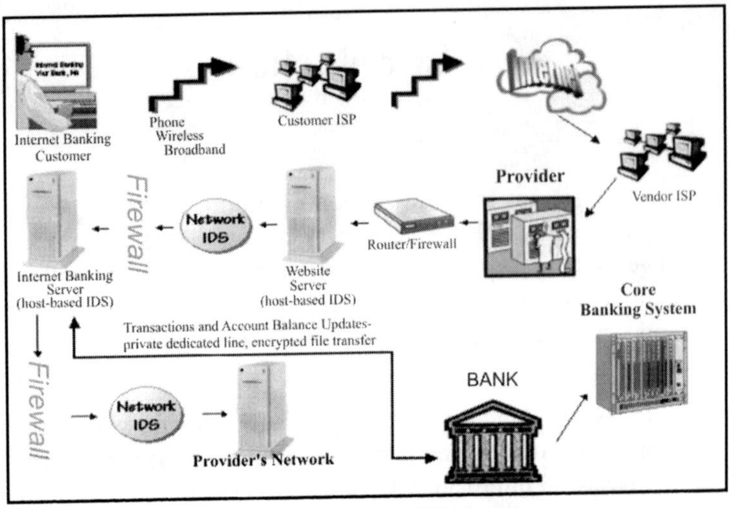

Figure 1 : Processing of E-Banking.

Difference Between Traditional Banking and E-Banking

Traditional Banking	E-Banking
1. In Traditional banking the customer has to visit the branch of the bank in person to perform the basic banking operations Viz., accounts enquiry, funds transfer, cash withdrawals, etc.	1. E-banking enables the customers to perform the basic banking transactions by sitting at their office or at home through PC or Laptop. The customers having an access to the banks website for viewing their account details and perform the transactions on account as per their requirements.
2. The brick and mortar structure of a bank is essential to perform banking functions.	2. With E-Banking, the brick and mortar structure of traditional banking gets converted into a click and portal model thereby giving a concept of virtual or innovative banking a real shape.
3. These are confined to Branches with less delivery channels.	3. E-Banking is no longer confined branches. Customers are being provided with additional delivery of channels which are more convenient to the customers and are cost effective to the banks. These

(Contd...)

	delivery channels include ATM, Tele Banking, Internet Banking, Mobile Banking, Home Banking, etc.
4. Banking transactions are conducted only in the banking hours and that too in the same building.	4. E-Banking facilities banking transactions by the customers round the clock globally.
5. Traditional banking is an art.	5. E-Banking is more of a science than art. E-Banking is knowledge based and mostly scientific in using the electronic devices of the computer revolution when most corporate tend to become internet working organizations, banking has to be E- Banking in the new century.

Aspects of E-Banking

E-Banking means the conduct of banking operations electronically. It calls for elimination of paper based transactions and radical change in the banking operations. E-banking will operate through internet, extranet and internet. E-banking is, therefore, a banking on the information super high ways on the frontier of the internet. E-banking must have the following dimensions.

(i) Easy Access to Customers: E-Banking is basically Internet based. Banking products and services such as deposits, remittances, credit cards, etc., as well as all important banking information can be made available with easy access to customers on internet. Thus, E-banking is a customer-to-bank service. Customers can make use of these services with no restricted office hours, no queues, no tellers and no waiting. Several network innovations for E-banking can be visualised such as smart card, electronic data, interchange, etc. Of course, the banking operations have to be guarded against unauthorised access by intruders.

(ii) Inter-bank Transactions: This form of electronic banking is for transacting inter-bank transactions such as money-at-call etc. In other words, it is a bank-to-bank service. This type of E-banking is driving extranets, which is restricted to banks only. Hence, it is well secured and unauthorised access is less.

(iii) Electronic Central Banking: Under electronic central banking, all banks, within the purview of a central bank, are interconnected on extranet to facilitate clearing of cheques, management of cash reserves, open market operations, discounting of bills etc. In fact, the Central Bank has to be connected with the government treasury on extranet to carry out its functions as an agent of the government. Again, the central banks of all the countries can be inter-linked with IMF, World Bank and other international financial institutions through extranets.

(iv) Intranet Procurement: For the transactions that are internal to a bank, between the banks and its branches and subsidiaries, Intranet procurements of banking is required. On the other hand, Extranet permits a bank to have full control over die users of intranet and the information to be transmitted.

The Extranet-Intranet-Internet relationship that exists in the process of E-banking has been shown in the following figure:

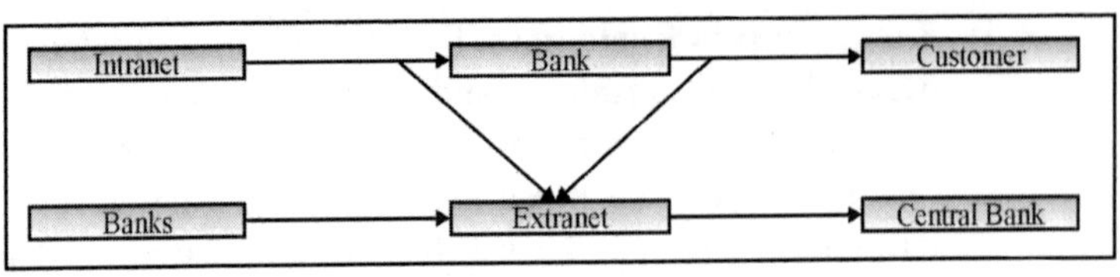

Figure 2: Micro Model of E-Banking.

Extensive work is required to integrate internal and external communication of bank-related information through banking internet and intranet for the development of the financial sector.

Significance of E-banking

E-Banking has the following advantages:

(i) Convenient Banking: E-banking increases the customer's convenience. No personal visit to the branch is required. Customers can perform basic banking transactions by simply sitting at their office or at home through PC or LAPTOP. Customers can get drafts at their doorsteps through email. Thus, E-banking facilitates home banking.

(ii) **Quality Banking:** E-banking opens new vests for providing efficient, economic and quality service to the customers. It allows the possibility of improved quality and an enlarged range of services being made available to customers.

(iii) **Round the Clock Banking:** E-banking facilitates performing of basic banking transactions by customers round the clock globally. World-wide 24 hours and 7 days a week banking services are made possible. In fact, there are no restricted office hours for E-banking.

(iv) **Service Banking:** E-banking creates strong basic infrastructure for the banks to embark upon many cash management products and to venture in the new fields like E-commerce, FDI etc. Instant credit, one day credit, immediate payment of utility bills, instant transfer offunds etc; would be made possible under E-banking. In short, it adds convenience to the entire banking services apart from widening the range of services.

(v) **Low Cost Banking (Service):** With the coming into existence of E-banking, the operational costs have come down due to technology adoption. The cost of transactions through internet banking is much less than any other traditional mode.

(vi) **Low Cost Banking (Establishment):** Brick and mortar structure of banking gets converted into click and Portal banking. Banks can have access to a greater number of potential customers without the commitment costs of physically opening branches. Thus, there is much saving on the cost of infrastructure. Moreover, requirements of staff at the banks get reduced to a greater extent.

(vii) **Speed Banking:** The increased speed of response to customer requirements under E-banking will lead to a greater customer satisfaction and handling a larger number of transactions at a lesser time. Thus, it increases the customers' convenience to a greater extent and facilitates better customer retention.

(viii) Profitable Banking: The increased speed of response to customer requirements under E-banking vis-à-vis branch banking can increase satisfaction and, consequently can lead to higher profits via handling a large number of customer accounts. Banks can also offer many cash management products for the existing customers without any additional cost.

From the above it is clear that E-banking has showered many benefits to the customers, banking system and others.

Impediments of E-banking

Although E-banking has provided many advantages, however, the following factors contribute as major constraints in the smooth implementation of E-banking:

(1) Initial Cost: Many banks have expressed their concern about the huge initial start-upcost for entering into E-banking. The start-up cost includes the following: (i) The connection cost to the internet or any other mode of electronic communication. The network should be robust, secured, efficient and scalable with inbuilt redundancy; (ii) The cost of sophisticated hardware, software and other related components including Modem, Routers, Bridges, Network Management system etc.; (iii) The cost of maintenance of all equipments, websites, skill level of employees etc.; (iv) The cost of setting up organisational activities to implement E-banking.

For a successful E-banking, bankers need to develop a coherent perspective of the role of network technologies and advancement of their EFT-departments with a competitive introspection of their banking business.

(2) Training and Retention of Staff: The introduction of E-banking involves 24 hours support environment, quality service to end-users and other partners which would necessitate a well-qualified and robust group of skilled persons to meets external and internal commitments. Hence, the bank has to spend a huge amount on their training. In this connection, what is more important is their retention in the organisation after imparting necessary training. Moreover, the bank has to outsource certain functions and services to maintain the level of standards and state of readiness. The training and retaining of skilled manpower is a major source of concern.

(3) **Shortage of Skilled Personnel:** It is a well known fact that there is scarcity of web developers, content providers and knowledgeable professionals to route banking transactions through internet. In a fast changing technological scenario, the obsolescence of technology is fast and hence there is always a paucity of skilled personnel.

(4) **Restricted Business:** All the transactions cannot be carried out electronically. Many deposits and some withdrawals require the use of postal services. Some banks have automated their front-end process for the customers, but still largely depend upon manual processes at the backend. For example, the Internet customers receive their statements online, but paper statements are also sent by mail. Mail and distribution costs are still necessary as the statements, cheques etc. are still mailed.

(5) **Restricted Clientele and Technical Problems:** The user of E-banking needs a computer and time to log on the site. It means that target clientele is restricted to those who have a home PC or can access the 'Net' through the office or cyber-cafes. Moreover, phone connections are not always perfect and, on a home PC, the modern connection often breaks off, requiring another tedious log-on. Navigating around websites on home computers is often slow and frustrating. Moreover, local calls are not free generally and so the customer has to pay everytime he checks his balance.

(6) **Legal Issues:** Legal framework for recognising the validity of banking transactions conducted through 'Net' is still being

- **Encryption Controls:** These controls are needed to enable those who possess secret key to decrypt the cyber text.

Innovative Banking (E-banking and Virtual Banking) in India

In India, till the 'eighties', the banks were operating in a protective environment characterised by administered interest rates, high level of pre-emptions in the form of reserve requirements and directed credit. **Banking sector reforms** were initiated in 1992 against the backdrop challenges faced by Indian banks from within and outside the banking system in the country as well as forces of globalisations operating world-wide. The accent to the reform process was to improve productivity and efficiency of the financial system.

Keeping in view this reform process the introduction of Innovative Banking was initiated. Introduction of information technology and communications networking system was set to change the operating environment of the banks drastically. Technology has already enabled some of the banks to introduce innovative products to their customers in the form of ATM facility, tele banking, home banking, 'any time' and 'anywhere' banking etc. While introducing innovative banking the following efficiency motives have been considered.

- **Organisational Structure:** With a view to reaping full benefits of liberalisation, the organisational structure of the banks need to be studied carefully. In this context, the chain of command needs to be shortened with adequate authority delegated to the branches. This would also help to enhance efficiency.
- **Adoption of Proper International Systems:** In addition to the organisational structure, adoption of proper internal systems and methods can greatly help in efficient functioning of the banks.
- **Human Resource Development:** Another issue that assumes importance in improving the efficiency of the banks is the human resource development. Recruiting the right people, training/retraining them on a continuous basis, keeping in

view the changing government and increasing complexities and having a remuneration/incentive structure conductive to keeping their moral high, are considered integral part of the process.

- **Consumer Service:** Another significant motive determining the efficiency and competitiveness is the customer service. The realisation that customer service satisfaction is essential for survival and growth has dawned on all the banks. The banks that will emerge as the winners in the impending era will be truly customer-centric banks.

Progress: With reference to the above context it may be mentioned that Virtual Banking has made some beginning in the Indian banking system, (i) ATMs have been installed by almost all the major banks in major metropolitan cities, (ii) The shared payment Network system (SPNS) has already been installed in Mumbai and (iii) Electronic Funds Transfer (EFT) mechanism by major banks has also been inititated. (iv) The operationalisation of the Very Small Aperture Terminal (VSAT) is expected to provide a significant thrust to the development of Indian Financial-NET Work (INFINET) which will further facilitate connectivity within the financial sector.

The popularity which virtual banking services have won among customers, owing to the speed, convenience and round-the-clock access they offer, is likely to increase in the future. However, several issues of concern would need to be pro-actively attended. While most of electronic banking have built-in security features such as encryption, prescriptions of maximum monetary limits and authorisations, the system operators have to be extremely vigilant and provide clear-cut guidelines for operations. On the larger issue of electronically initiated funds transfer, issues like authentication of payments instructions, the responsibility of the customer for secrecy of the security procedure would also need to be addressed.

Main Instruments or Facilities Provided by E-banking / Innovative Banking

- **Computerisation:** Now-a-days almost all banks have computerised their operations. Besides, all banks in different countries are inter-linked with each other through internet. This mechanism has facilitated easy remittance of money not only inside the country but also to any part of the world through the press of button. Money can be, transferred from one account in one branch to another account in another branch of the same bank or a different bank.

After the introduction of computers, M.T. (Mail Transfer) and T.T. (Telegraphic Transfer) have lost their significance. It is so because computers have facilitated speedy remittance of funds from one end to another in a moments notice. Thus, it minimizes the loss of interest since money is transferred instantly from one end to another. Moreover, it facilitates transfer of money from one branch of a bank to another branch of a different bank also which is not possible in the case of M.T. or T.T.

Recently arrangements have been made to pass on messages either general or specific through Satellite facility. For instance banks all over the world are inter-linked with satellite maintained by SWIFT (Society for Worldwide Inter-bank Financial Telecommunications) in Europe. In India, Gateway, Bombay, maintained by the computer Maintenance Corporation of India is its agent. Those banks which want to enjoy this satellite facility in India can open SWIFT centres with Gateway, and thus, all the banks in the world are inter-linked with each other. Any general information like foreign exchange rate movements or specific information like remittance of money, or opening of Letter of Credit or making forfeiting arrangements can be passed on to the banks concerned or to all the banks as a whole as the case may be in a moment's notice through this satellite arrangement.

Banks have also introduced mechanised cheque clearance using magnetic ink character recognition (MICR) technology. Banks are also in the process of setting up exclusive data communication network for banks known as BANKNET. Banks are now switching to Personal Computers (PCs) and LAN/VAN systems. The Reserve Bank has put-in place Electronic Funds Transfer (EFT) system, Delivery Vs. Payment (DVP), Electronic Clearing Services (ECS) and RBINET. It has also taken steps to set up a Very Small Aperture Terminal (VSAT) Network which will cover all banks and financial institutions to serve as a number of tasks like MIS, data warehousing, transaction processing, currency chest accounting, ATMs, EFT, EDT, Smart/ Credit cards, etc,. It will cover 2,800 centres soon.

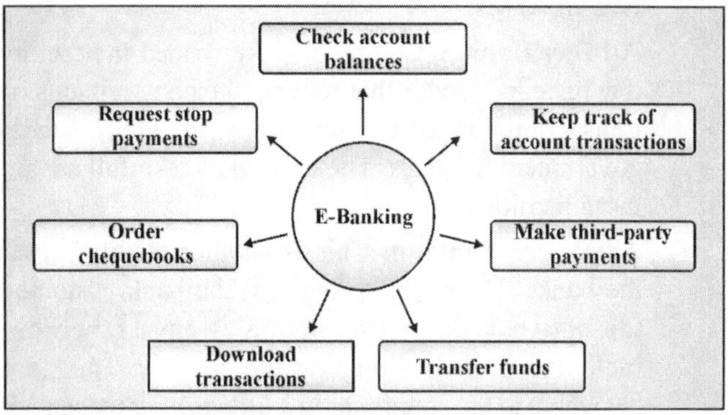

Figure 3: Model of E-Banking.

- **ATM Facility:** The introduction of Automated Tellers Machines facility is an important step in the banking sector. The leading banks of the country have established ATMs, not only in their head offices but also at the branches, to provide twenty four services to their customers so that they

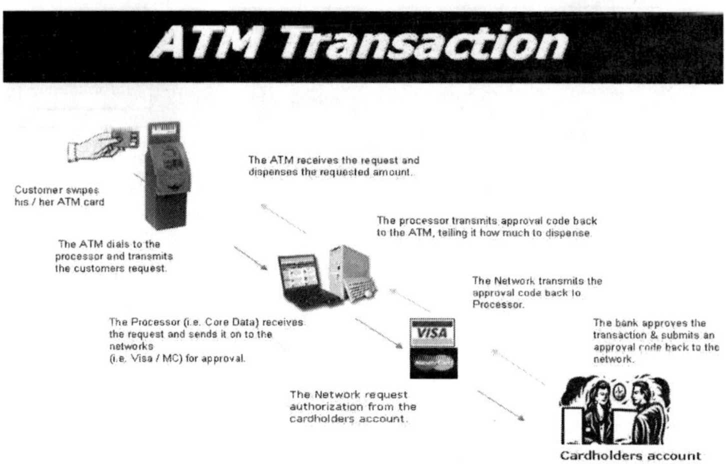

Figure 4: Process of Using ATM Machine.

may be able to have transactions in money. The customer, who possesses the ATM card, can go to the ATM branch of the bank and can withdraw any amount from his deposited money. He can also deposit any amount in the bank with the help of ATMs.

- **All Day Banking:** Some banks provided the facility of all day banking. Under this scheme the bank remains open for transactions on all the seven day, including sundays and government holidays. The customers take full advantage of these facilities.
- **Anywhere Banking:** This is another facility provided by the banks. Under this provision, the bank customers have the option to have transaction at any branch or place, including branches outside the country. Thus, a person anywhere in the country or in a foreign country can withdraw or deposit his/her money with the branch of the bank, where he has account.
- **Net Banking or 'On Line Banking':** In the field of information technology, the internet has brought a tremendous revolution all over the world. The banking sector has also not remained untouched by it. The internet has helped

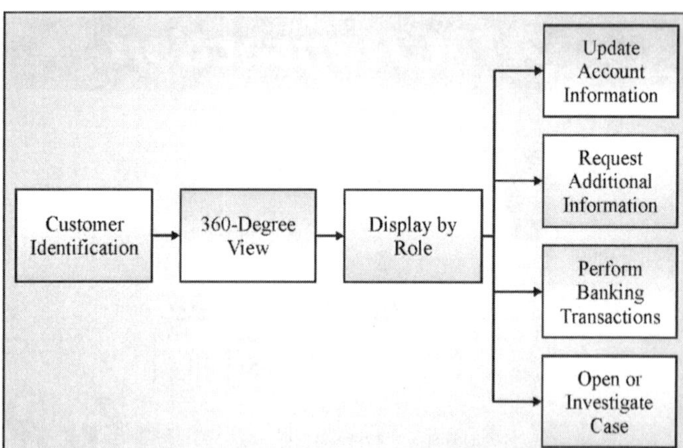

Figure 5 : Net Banking Technology.

the banking sector to provide its services very rapid and fast. This new or changed form of providing this fast service is known as Net Banking or 'On Line Banking'.

Under Net Banking, the customer is not required to go to any counter of the bank. He has simply to open his Personal Computer (PC) will click the website of the bank, put down his account card there, do the entry of some of his transactions (deposits and withdrawals) and will do O.K. by pressing enter. Further the bank will do the needful job. Thus, the concerned customer, in this way, will be able to finish his job in minutes rather than in hours and will be able to save his labour and cost.

The Net Banking is not only fast but also cheaper. A study in U.S.A. reveals that the cost of operation of the account in Net Banking one-fifth of a dollar. Further the Net Banking has also broken the geographical boundaries. You can now operate your account anywhere in the world and can transfer your money within no time. Money deposited in a foreign bank in any foreign country can be collected in any city in India through internet or 'On Line Banking'. Thus, the future of 'Net Banking' is very bright in an underdeveloped country like India.

Net Banking is very popular in European countries and U.S.A., where it started functioning about 15 years back. But in India its origin is recent and it is considered to be the gift of millennium. The banks who have started network, are ICICI Bank, Global Tourist Bank, IDBI, and some other banks. The public sector banks are also preparing themselves to come in this field. So far State Bank of India, Canara Bank, Union Bank, etc. Have initiated their functioning in this direction. Besides the Indian branches of foreign banks have also providing this facility.

- **Mobile Banking or M-Banking:** Mobile Banking or M-banking refers to that of banking system where a person, sitting miles away, can enquire and check his saving account and can do transactions with the help of his mobile phone. The beginning of M-banking is a significant step from the side of Innovative Banking.

Figure 6 : Benefits of Mobile Banking.

Here it may be mentioned that a beginning has been made for converting internet portels into mortels for this technological change. The internet service givers, Cellular Operators, Telecommunication companies, E-Commerce Enablers, Mobile Phone Manufacturers and Networking Companies have engaged themselves to shape their basic structure into wireless form. HDFC, IDBI and ICICI have already given a wireless to their infrastructure.

Operational Process of Mobile Banking: In M-banking the customer sends his message to the bank through his cell-phone by using short-cut Messaging Service (SMS) technology. Within 12 to 18 seconds the answer of the message is received on the screen of the cell-phone. This service is available both for the credit card holders and bank account. The services included in it are present balance in the customer's account, order for the stoppage of payment on a cheque and the changes in the credit limit of the account. The customer has only to type the standard keywords on his cell-phone such as 'I' for IDBI bank, 'CCHQ,' for cheque book, 'BAL' for balance. Suppose your Bank is IDBI, then for knowing your balance you have to type 'IBAL' in your cell-phone. Thus, this type of facility is available to a customer during his travel, or without coining over to the bank he comes to know the details of his financial position.

The speedy growth of M-banking is the need of the time. More hopes are also centralised on mobile phones, because mobile phone holders are more in number in the country as compared to Personal Computer (PC) and LAPTOP holders. The other merit of mobile phone is that one can carry it along with him/her, whereas the PC and LAPTOP cannot be carried anywhere and everywhere.

A question-mark which is attached to both the Mobile banking or Online banking is the problem or question of security i.e. the fear of hacking and tempering of data. Secrecy is the essence of banking transactions. The security products both hardware based on application software based, should address the twin issues of taking care of customers interests and also ensure secure funds transfer.

- **Wireless Application Protocol (WAP):** Cellular phone operators are forwarding towards the new technology of wireless Application Protocol. This is an important step towards converting information- based service to transaction based service. Thus, WAP is a technique which helps banking transaction with the help of mobile phone. WAP is such a standard which makes it possible for internet access through WAP-enabled instruments and mobile phone, Palm Top, Personal Digital Assistant, Digital Diary etc. SMS is similar to that of E-mail whereas WAP provides internet on mobile phone. Although SMS is considered to be cheap and slow-speed service yet WAP is more favourable to customers, because it makes the real transaction possible and graphics can be downloaded in it. In this context ICICI has already started an other interesting banking service known as **'Bill junction Com'** and the ICICI bank claims it is a first Online Bill presentation and payment service.

The WAP website provides all the account holders of the banks the facility to present their respective electricity, water and telephone bills on the internet and also provides the service of payment: through their bank accounts.

Critics are of the opinion that Online Banking or Net-Banking has the chance of more success as compared to WAP banking. In support of their opinion they are argue that M-banking will consume more time of the consumers and also not more comfortable to the customers because the screen size of the mobile phone cannot be enhanced.

- **Credit Cards:** Banks have recently introduced the credit card system. Credit cards are issued to good customers having a certain minimum income and having current or saving accounts, free of charge. The credit card enables a customer to purchase goods or services from certain retail and service establishments upto certain limit without making immediate payment. The establishments get paid by the bank operating the plan. The bank assumes the risk and responsibility of

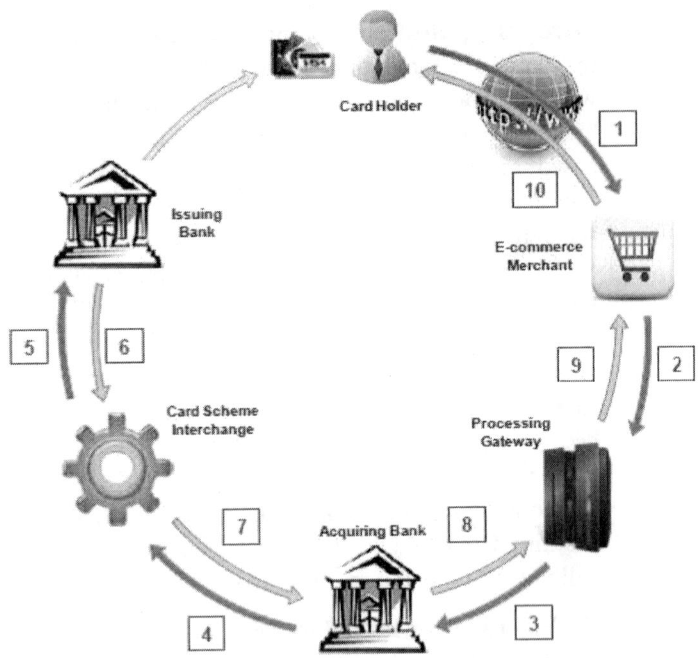

Figure 7 : Credit Card Transaction Model.

collecting the dues from the customers. Here it may be mentioned that the card holder is required to pay neither an interest to the bank nor a higher price for goods purchased; he pays only a fee to the bank for the facility. Thus, through credit cards the banks have found the way of deploying the surplus /unused funds; thereby they have started gaining by interest, service charges etc.

The cost of arrangement is met from the increased sales which result from the use of the credit cards. The card issuing bank pays to the seller as soon as goods are sold but charges the buyer after 30 to 45 days. The bank also bears the risk that the card holder might default. For all this, the bank get commission from the seller which is about 2.5 to 5 percent of the value of goods sold. The gain of the bank is the extent of commission from the seller minus the risk and interest factors, and administrative and advertising expenses. In addition the banks earn by way of initial, annual, add-on and re-issue fees from the prospective card holders. There are significant differences in the fees charged by different banks. The cards are usually used by elite corporate executives, businessmen, persons belonging to middle income groups and so on. They are usually used to buy consumer durables and certain services at establishments such as shops, hospitals, nursing homes, departmental stores, hotels, railways, petrol stations and so on.

Operational Procedure of Credit Cards: Each credit card bears the specimen signature of the holder and is embossed by the issuing banker with the holder's name and address. The establishments, on presentation of the card, delivers the goods or provides the services. The supplier places the card in a special ink printer machine to record the holder's name and number on a sales voucher to which are added the particulars of the transaction. The holders signs the voucher and the signature is compared by the supplier with that on the card. The voucher is then sent to the bank which pays it after deducting its service charges. Once in a month, the bank sends a statement of all the credit purchase in the previous month to the credit holder and the latter has to remit the amount either by cash or by cheque.

Credit through Credit Cards: The competition in the banking industry in marketing cards provides ample opportunity to consumers in making use of credit/debit cards. The opportunity created by this chance contributes to consumers making credit card choices without giving much weightage to the high probability that they will pay interest on their outstanding balances. Consumers pay a little or no attention to the risk involved with credit cards for the sake of ease of use and hope that they will have the time and ultimately the money to pay off their cumulated credit.

Although credit cards are available with interest rates ranging from 9 percent to 15 percent, most of the consumers use credit cards with interest rates as high as 18 percent or more. Another important factor that consumers don't consider much is that the annual fees/ service charges vary from bank to bank. These factors could make a significant difference to the use of the credit cards by consumers. In addition, some customers are ignorant about how to transfer balances from cards with higher rates to cards with lower rates. Consequently, major credit card issuers are persistently earning from three to five times the ordinary rate of return in banking.

Credit Cards Create Credit: Though credit cards replace the use of cash and provide overdraft facility and additional borrowing power, the cardholders can make use of such facilities only if they agree to pay interest and other charges. The spending power of the cardholder depends on the drawing capacity. Credit cards are the key to the opening of bank account for daily payment by the cardholder. Overdraft facility is also available in the range of Rs 2000 to Rs 10,000 or more, depending upon the credit worthiness of the cardholder.

Objectives of the Study

- To study and analyze Growth, Trends and Emerging Issues of E- Banking services in India.
- To determine Customer Perception and Employee Perception of selected Public Sector Banks and Private Sector Banks towards E-Banking services.

- To examine the Productivity of selected Public Sector Banks and Private Sector Banks which are providing E-Banking services.
- To assess the Profitability of selected Public Sector Banks and Private Sector Banks which are providing E-Banking services.
- To calculate the Co-efficient & Correlation between Productivity, Profitability and Customer Satisfaction.
- To prepare a model which contains Micro Economic Variable to enhance the customer satisfaction of E-Banking services.
- To determine usage and reasons for preferring e-banking services.
- To have an insight into the attitudes and behaviours of customers.
- Studying the psychological aspects of Indian customers which stop them from shifting towards internet banking.
- Suggesting ways for making E-Banking in India successful.

Research Hypothesis

It is indeed essential to emphasize the fact that the Indian culture is different from the countries where previous research was conducted. The researchers predicted that the familiarity and economic benefits of using the Internet has a significant impact on the acceptance of online banking. If the customers are not used to accessing the Internet frequently, and if they do not trust the Internet as a secure environment to conduct financial transactions, then it is nearly impossible for them to accept online banking. Therefore, the following hypotheses were adopted:

Following are the Hypothesis for the study

- H0 = There is no difference in satisfaction level in Public and Private sector Banks.
- H1 = There is significant difference in satisfaction level in Public and Private sector Banks.
- H0 = All the selected attributes effect customer satisfaction equally.

- H1 = All the selected attributes effect customer satisfaction inequally.
- H0 = There is no relationship between age and use of Internet banking can reduce the number of physical visit to bank.
- H1 = There is relationship between age and use of Internet banking can reduce the number of physical visit to bank.
- H0 = There is no relationship between occupation and use of internet banking can reduce the number of physical visit to bank.
- H1 = There is relationship between occupation and use of internet banking can reduce the number of physical visit to bank.
- H0 = There is relationship between education and use of Internet banking can reduce the number of physical visit to bank.
- H1 = There is no relationship between education and use of internet banking can reduce the number of physical visit to bank.

Research Methodology

The following are the research method used by the researcher:

Research Design: Descriptive Research.

Sources of Data:

Primary Data- Various banks respondents using e-banking services and the information about the selected bank is gathered from the discussion with the employees of bank. For data collection, observation and interview method is used. Interview of manager can be conduct to get information.

Secondary Data- (Published Data) The secondary data was collected from summary reports, e-mails, circulars, books, notifications of RBI and an annual report of the bank.

Population: E-Banking users of selected Public and Private Sector Banks. Sampling: Sampling may be defined as selection of some part of an aggregate or totality on the basis of which a judgment or interface about the aggregate or totality is made.

A. **Sampling Design:** A Sampling design is a definite plan for obtaining a sample given Population. There is different method of the sampling. Here Random & Stratified sampling technique has been used.

B. **Sample size:** This refers to the number of the items to be selected from the universe to constitute a sample. There are 300 + 300 sample respondent are taken as a sample size who are using traditional and internet banking.

C. **Sampling Frame:** For study sampling frame includes internet banking users like businessman, professionals, and salaried person etc.

D. **Data collection instruments:** A data is collected with structured questionnaire.

Limitations of the Study

The following are the limitations of the study:

- The proposed study will concentrate only on qualitative aspects.
- Random and Stratified sampling technique likely to be applied in the selection of bank customers.
- E-banking promotes lack of socialising/social contacts.
- Hackers may intercept data and defraud customers.
- Phone bills can increase.
- Customers will be more vulnerable to phishing.
- Customers are compelled to have computers at home, Internet access and computer skills.

Introduction to E-Banking 26

REFERENCES

1. Adams, D.A., Nelson, R.R., Todd, RA. (1992), "Perceived usefulness, ease of use, and usage of information technology: a replication", *MIS Quarterly,* No. June, pp. 227-47.

2. Davis, F.D., Bagozzi, R.P, Warshaw, P.R.(1989), "User acceptance of computer technology: a comparison of two theoretical models", *Management Science,* Vol. 35, No. 8, pp. 982-1003.
3. Gerrard, P, Cunningham, J.B. (2003), "The diffusion of Internet banking among Singapore consumers", *The International Journal of Bank Marketing,* Vol. 21 No.l, pp. 16-28.
4. Igbaria, M., Livari, J., & Maragahh, H.(1995), Why do individuals use computer technology? A Finnish case study. *Information & Management,* 29, 227-238.
5. Kasheir, D., Ashour, S.A., Yacout, M. O. (2009), "Factors Affecting Continued Usage of Internet Banking Among Egyptian Customers", Communications of the IBIMA, Vol. 9, No. 29, pp. 252-263.
6. Magi, A.W. (2003), "Share of Wallet in Retailing: The Effects of Customer Satisfaction, Loyalty Cards and Shopper Characteristics," *Journal of Retailing,* Vol. 79, No. 2, pp. 97-106.
7. Mishra, A. K, "Internet Banking in India PartfF, available at: http://www.banknetindia.com/banking/ibkg.htm
8. Singh and Malhotra (2004), "Status of Internet Banking in India", *Management Accountant,* Vol. 39, No. II, pp. 890-896.
9. Sulaiman, A., Lim, C.H., and Wee, A. (2005), "Prospects and Challenges of E-Banking in Malaysia", *Electronic Journal on Information Systems in Developing Countries,* Vol. 22, No. l, pp. 1-11.
10. Wang, Y., Wang, Y., Lin, H., Tang, T., 2003. Determinants of user acceptance of Internet banking: an empirical study. *Int. J. Serv. Ind. Manage.* 14 (5), 501–519.
11. Wungwanitchakorn, A., 2002. Adoption intention of banks' customers on Internet banking service. *ABAC J.* 22 (3), 63–80.
12. Xue, M., Hitt, L.M., Chen, P.Y., 2011. Determinants and outcomes of Internet banking adoption. *Manage. Sci.* 57 (2), 291–307.

Chapter - II

Review of Literature

In order to reap the benefits of having loyal customers and gaining a competitive advantage online, companies need to develop a thorough understanding of the antecedents of loyalty on the World Wide Web (e-loyalty), such as business factors [Bhattacherjee, 2001] or personal characteristics [Magi, 2003]. In order to investigate the importance of e-loyalty, the identification of variables influencing repeat purchasing behaviour and word-of-mouth recommendation is a crucial area of research [Srinivasan *et al.,* 2002]. This holds especially true for those industries which already depend heavily on their reputations and long-lasting relationships in the offline world, as is the case with the financial sector. The widespread adoption of online banking services calls for research investigating those factors which are responsible for keeping customers loyal.

A model explaining the antecedents of loyalty in the online banking industry has to incorporate factors which take into account the characteristics of the industry as well as those of the medium. Therefore, we consider antecedents such as trust (being important online and offline) and the perceived quality of the Web site (being important only online). Besides being topics of scholarly research in the information systems domain, these issues have been long discussed in marketing. More than two decades have passed since the concept of relationship marketing was first mentioned in the marketing literature [Berry, 1983], Drivers such as intense competition, demanding customers and enablers such as the Internet are the reason why relationship marketing has increasingly attracted the attention of researchers and practitioners alike [Sheth and Parvatiyar, 2002].

In relationship marketing research the concept of customer loyalty plays a central role [Christopher *et al.,* 2004], The preeminent importance of retaining customers is supported by several studies [Chen *et al.,* 2002], confirming the relevance of customers' loyalty to a firm's profitability. New forms of online communication offer a host of new and promising opportunities for customer retention on the World Wide Web, while at the same time intensifying competition [Vatanasombut *et al.,* 2004], In particular, this applies to company-controlled communication, giving companies the ability to customize information with regard to the individual needs of a particular customer and to optimise the customer's feedback opportunities [Kierzkowski *et al.,* 1996. At the same time, companies also face completely new challenges arising from customer-controlled.

Review of Bygone Studies

The E-Banking Sector:

Online banking, which can be defined as the provision of information or services by a bank to its customers over the Internet [Daniel, 1999], has been one of the major developments in the financial service sector in recent years. According to a survey conducted by Pew Internet and America Life, online banking has been the fastest growing Internet activity in the US over the last five years. As of November 2004, a total of 53 million Americans (44% of all US Internet users) use some form of online banking service [McGann, 2005].

In Germany, the number of online accounts has increased almost tenfold between 1999 and 2004, with 40% of all accounts now being online [Association of German Banks, 2004].

A short review of the literature on electronic banking briefly illustrates the major issues that researchers and practitioners have dealt with in recent years. Security turned out to be a major obstacle for many customers who were otherwise willing to switch to the online world [Martin, 1998]. Besides assuring customers that their privacy is protected, Hamlet [2000] suggests that banks should not over-animate or clutter their Web sites with too much advertising.

In addition, care should be taken not to over-personalise the online-experience in order to avoid the impression that personal financial information is freely available. Bhattacherjee [2001] uses online banking customers to test his expectation-confirmation model of IS continuance. His results suggest that users' continuance intention is determined by their satisfaction and perceived usefulness of the application. Table 1 shows a number of research papers that empirically validate models in the context of e-banking. Tan and Teo [2000] found that attitudinal factors such as Internet experience, the relative advantage of online banking and perceived risk, and perceived behavioural control factors predict the intention to adopt Internet banking services. The survey by Karjaluoto *et al.* [2002] showed that prior experience with computers and technology as well as people's attitudes toward computers influences both their attitude toward online banking and their actual behaviour. Mukherjee and Nath [2003] found that communication had a moderate influence on trust, while opportunistic behaviour had a significant negative effect and trust in general led to a higher level of commitment in online banking. Information sharing and distrust in the Internet were identified as the two major drawbacks for Thai Internet banking adoption by Rotchanakitumnuai and Speece [2004]. Based on a survey amongst Finnish banking customers, Pikkarainen *et al.* [2004] found perceived usefulness and information on online banking on the Website to be the main drivers for the acceptance of online banking. A recent study by Lassar *et al.* [2005] showed that Internet related innovativeness is positively related to the adoption of online banking.

With the number of online banking consumers steadily increasing, the focus of attention shifts from enticing customers to the online world to retaining them. While the focus of the aforementioned papers lies on offline versus online, this paper deals with the problem of how to keep a customer online and loyal to a specific supplier. Therefore, we analyze which antecedents might induce customers to stay with a particular online bank instead of switching suppliers. We will start discussing our model by referring to the concept of loyalty, which has been investigated extensively in the offline world.

Chakravarty (1996) illustrated that Banking, being a customer-oriented services industry, the customer is the centre of attention and customer service has to be the distinguishing factor. The challenge for banks is to lower costs, increase efficiency, while improving the quality of their service, and increase customer satisfaction. Attention has now turned to improving the quality of service encounter, when customers enter the bank and come into face-to-face contact with bank staff.

Birch and Young (1997) analyzed the consumer side for e-banking and the results showed that consumers basically seek for transactional efficiency, choice for core and non-core banking products and access to competitive prices and returns.

Filotto *et al.* (1997) illustrated that the adoption rates of ATM were higher among young users. In addition, Barnett (1998) findings proved that younger consumers are more comfortable in using e-banking. Katz and Aspden (1997) findings explained that males were more likely to adopt e-banking than females. Mookerji (1998) explored that internet banking is fast becoming popular in India. Nevertheless, it is still in its evolutionary stage. They expect that a large sophisticated and highly competitive internet banking market will develop in future.

Girish V, Preetha S (1997) in his paper on "Technology in banks - A global perspective" he argued that technology in banks would help to increase the level of productivity and customer satisfaction. To meet the challenges posed by the entry of foreign banks, Indian banks will have to invest heavily in technology to meet competition, reduce cost, improve customer service, improve productivity and offer new products/services.

Sathye (1997) reviewed the status of internet banking in Australia. The study found that only two of the 52 banks started internet banking services. He opined that education would be a crucial factor for expanding internet banking in Australia. If customers are convinced about the various advantages of internet banking they will start asking for this service from their banks, and will put pressure on the banks to go ahead with internet banking.

Daniel (1999) defines electronic banking as the delivery of banks' information and services by banks to customers via different delivery platforms that can be used with different terminal devices such as a personal computer and a mobile phone with browser or desktop software, telephone or digital television. Electronic banking is commonly known as E-banking. E-banking defined as "the delivery of banking services through the open-access computer network directly to customers' home or private address". Joseph *et al.* (1999) examined the influence of internet on the delivery of banking services. They found six primary dimensions of e-banking service quality such as convenience and accuracy, feedback and complaint management, efficiency, queue management, accessibility and customisation.

Mols (1999) acknowledged that the internet banking is an innovative distribution channel that offers less waiting time and a higher spatial convenience than traditional branch banking with significantly lower cost structure than traditional delivery channels. Internet banking reduces not only operational cost to the bank but also leads to higher levels of customer satisfaction and retention. As a result internet banking is very attractive to banks and consumers, who now have higher acceptance to new technology.

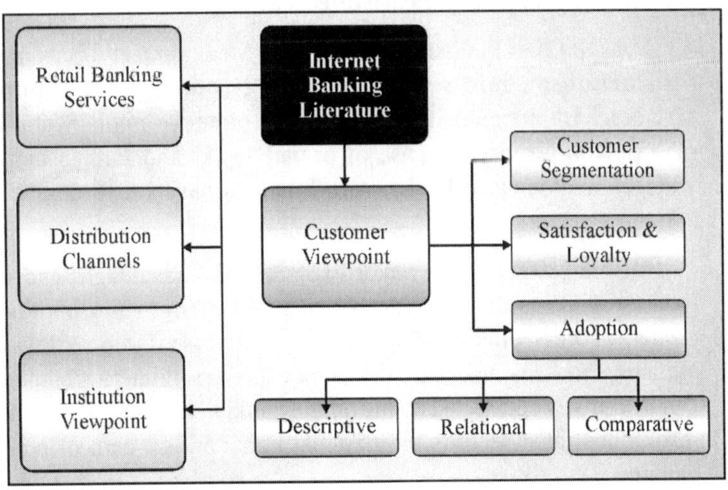

Figure 8 : Internet Banking Literature.

Jeevan (2000) observed that the internet banking enables banks to offer low cost and high value added financial services. US web-corporation argues that finally banks are finding that a comprehensive online banking strategy is indispensable for success in the increasingly competitive financial services market. Changes in technology, competition and lifestyles have changed the face of banking and banks in the present environment are looking for alternative ways to provide differentiated services.

Hasan (2002) found that online home banking has came out as a significant strategy for banks to attract and retain customers. About 75 percent of the Italian banks have adopted some form of internet banking during the period 1993-2000.

Simpson (2002) suggests that e-banking is driven largely by the prospects of operating costs minimisation and operating revenues maximisation. A comparison of online banking in developed and emerging markets reveal that in developed markets lower costs and higher revenues are more noticeable. Karjaluoto (2002) observed electronic banking is a construct that consists of several distribution channels. DeYoung (2005) analyze the performance of Internet- only banks versus the brick and mortars in the US market and find strong evidence of general experience effects available to all start ups.

Vyas, P (2004) in his paper entitled "Measurement of customer satisfaction on information technology adoption in banking services." He concluded that there was effective implementation of e-banking services in case of private banks and foreign banks, whereas, nationalised banks were found to have lesser degree of computerisation.

Mishra (2005) in his paper explained the advantages and the security concerns about internet banking. According to him, improved customer access, offering of more services, increased customer loyalty, attracting new customers are the primary drivers of internet banking. But in a survey conducted by the online banking association, member institutions rated security as the most important concern of online banking.

Shu, W. and Strassmann, P. A. (2005) in article on "Does information technology provide banks with profit?," he Studied 12 banks operating in the US for the period of 1989-1997 and found that although IT has been one of the most marginal productive factors among all inputs, it cannot increase banks' profits. On the other hand, there are some studies agreeing with the positive influence of IT spending to business value.

Kozak, S. (2005) in his article entitled "the role of information technology in the profit and cost efficiency improvements of the banking sector" he examines the impact of the progress in IT on the profit and cost efficiencies of the US banking sector during the period of 1992-2003. The research shows a positive correlation between the levels of implemented IT and both profitability and cost savings.

Nyangosi *et al.* (2009) collected customers' opinions regarding the importance of e-Banking and the adoption levels of different e-Banking technologies in India and Kenya. The study highlighted the trends of e-banking indicators in both countries. The overall result indicates that customers in both countries have developed a positive attitude and they give much importance to the emergence of e-banking.

From the review of literature, we found that education is one of the crucial factors for expanding e-banking. Younger consumers and males are more comfortable in using e-banking. Convenience and accuracy, feedback and complaint management, efficiency, queue management, accessibility and customisation were found to be primary dimensions of e-banking service quality. However, most of the studies are carried out in foreign countries. In the light of the above findings, the present study is undertaken in Indian context to find out bankers perspectives on e-banking and comparative study of selected Public and Private sector Banks.

Research Problem

Banks have transformed themselves and are offering services through internet. E-banking is defined as the automated delivery of new and traditional banking products and services directly to customers through electronic, interactive communication channels.

E-banking includes the systems that enable financial institution customers, individuals or businesses, to access accounts, transact business, or obtain information on financial products and services through a public or private network, including the Internet. Nowadays commercial banks more concentrate on the E-banking services and there is competition in between them. The customer of commercial banks also attract towards e-banking services hence the research paper is titled as **"A Critical Study of trends in E- Banking with Special References to Selected Public and Private Sector Banks."**

About the Problem

With the changing environment, banks implemented tele-banking, mobile banking and call centre services, ATM and others one after another. Due to rapid change in technology and the entry of private and foreign banks a number of new products and delivery channels have been introduced. Among the major initiatives Internet Banking has brought to the customers the much demanded convenience. The advent of internet banking offers banking firms a new frontier of opportunities and challenges. Despite these possibilities, there are various psychological and behavioural issues such as reluctance to change, trust in one's bank, security concerns, preference of human interference and the like impede the growth of internet banking. In this regard a study has been undertaken in Internet banking services provided by the selected Public and Private sector Banks.

Introduction

Banks have been developing new instruments and services and improving processes, both to reduce costs of existing services and to offer new services. The pace of innovation has increased dramatically particularly with the advances in information processing and communications technologies. Consequently, internet banking has changed the nature of consumer interactions with banks, reducing the importance of physical branch locations which involve face-to-face interactions. Many services are available now through the internet. Internet banking provides a convenient, low-cost alternative to the traditional bank visit. Internet banking in this study is defined as an internet portal, through which customers can use different kinds of banking services ranging from providing information and bill payment to making investments. Indian banks and their customers enjoy an array of benefits through adoption of internet banking. The Internet and Mobile Association of India report (IAMAI 2006) reveals that the costs of banking service through the Internet amount to a fraction of the costs through conventional methods. Industry estimates assume teller cost at Re 1 per transaction, ATM transaction costs at Re 0.45, phone banking at Re 0.35, debit cards at Re 0.20 and Internet banking at Re 0.10 per transaction.

On the whole, one can easily conclude that Internet banking increases operational efficiencies and reduces costs, besides giving a platform for offering value added services to the customer, thereby fulfilling all the essential prerequisites for a flourishing banking industry. In anticipation of efficiency in operating costs, banks seek the diffusion of internet banking. However, banks cannot expect instant returns, unless the Internet population itself reaches a critical mass.

On the customers' side also there are many advantages. First, there is twenty four hour access. And second, banks can be accessed from anywhere in the world at one's own convenience. Additionally there is time savings, convenience, increased access to information on their bank accounts and effective management of personal finances.

Although the advantages of internet banking seem to pull consumers towards its usage, the evidence for consumers' reluctance to use internet banking calls for a scholarly inquiry into the underlying factors influencing individual consumers' decision to adopt internet banking. Human beings, being creatures of habit will probably view anything that is new with caution and suspicion. The same applies to internet banking. People are cautious and often reluctant to depart from traditional ways of banking to internet banking. Crores of rupees have been spent on building Internet banking systems in India but reports show that potential users may not use the systems in spite of their availability.

This, points out the need for research to identify the factors that determine acceptance of Internet banking by the users. In India, comparatively less number of studies have been conducted on the current status of internet banking and internet banking adoption compared to other countries. Thus, there is a lot of scope for the research to present new ideas concerning internet banking in India which may be useful to the Indian banking industry.

There is a growing body of research focusing on examining the determinants of computer technology acceptance and utilisation among users (Moore and Benbasat, 1991; Saleh, 2003; Randolph, 2001). Several competing theoretical approaches have been used to investigate the determinants of acceptance and use of information technology (Venkatesh *et al,* 2003). Important lines of study in this area focus on the determinants of individual acceptance of new technologies by using actual behaviour itself (Davis, 1989; Taylor and Todd, 1995). These various theories explain technology acceptance and adoption. In acceptance studies, researchers focus on the attitudinal explanations of the use of a specific technology or service. The studies rely largely on the following five concepts: perceived user friendliness, perceived usefulness, attitudes towards use, intention to use and actual use.

Adoption research is grounded in three models from social psychology, namely, the Theory of Reasoned Action (TRA) (Ajzen and Fishbein, 1980), the Theory of Planned Behaviour (TPB) (Ajzen, 1991) and Technology Acceptance Model (TAM). Of the three theories, TAM has emerged as the most powerful and parsimonious theory to represent the antecedents of technology usage through belief in two factors that is, perceived usefulness and perceived ease of use of an information system (Davis, 1989). TAM has received empirical support in information technology research from many research studies regardless of the country concerned (Guriting and Nelson, 2006; Wang *et al.*, 2003; Ramayah and Ling, 2002; and Venkatesh and Morris, 2000). Given below is a brief description of the Technology Acceptance Model.

Technology Acceptance Model

The TAM is an adaptation of Theory of Reasoned Action (TRA) specifically tailored for modeling user acceptance of new information technology (software information systems within organisations) (Davis, 1989). While TRA suggests that social behaviour is motivated by an individual's attitude towards carrying out that behaviour, it does not specify what specific beliefs would be important in a particular situation. TAM posits that the actual usage of technology can be predicted by user's behavioural intention and his/her attitude towards use, which in turn are influenced by the technology's perceived ease of use and perceived usefulness. TAM adopts the well-established causal chain as follows:

Beliefs > Attitude > Intention > Behaviour

Davis (1989) used the Theory of Reasoned Action (TRA) and developed the Technology Acceptance Model (TAM). Based on certain beliefs, a person forms an attitude about certain objects, on the basis of which he forms an intention as to how he should behave with respect to that object. The intention to behave is the sole determinant of actual behaviour. Davis adapted the TRA by developing two key beliefs, perceived ease of use (PEOU) and perceived usefulness (PU) to determine individual's acceptance of a technology, more specifically information system usage. The first of

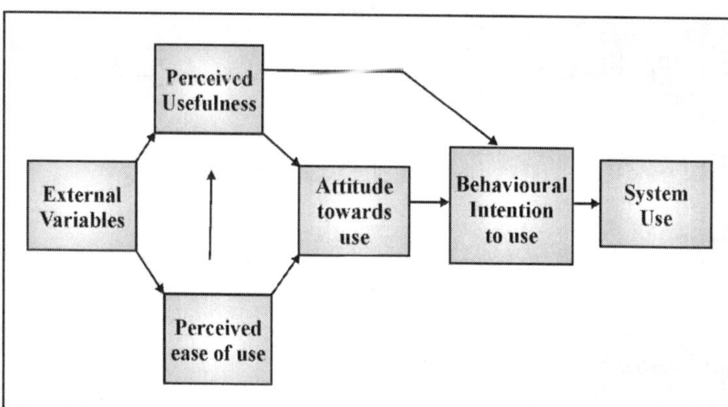

Figure 9 : The Technology Acceptance Model The Research Framework.

these beliefs perceived usefulness is defined as the 'degree to which a person believes that using a particular system would be beneficial or enhance his/her job performance' (Davis, 1989). The second, perceived ease of use is defined as 'the degree to which a person believes that using a particular system would be free of effort' (Davis, 1989). A diagram of the model is presented in Figure one.

The Research Framework

Considering the uniqueness of internet banking and its users, and the simplicity of the Technology Acceptance Model, an extended TAM is used as a theoretical framework to examine the effects of Computer self-efficacy on users' acceptance of internet banking through attitude towards internet banking, where attitude is influenced by three beliefs namely, Perceived usefulness, Perceived ease of use and Perceived security.

The research model tested is shown in Figure 2. It includes the individual difference variable 'Computer self-efficacy' and three belief variables (Perceived usefulness, Perceived ease of use and Perceived Security)

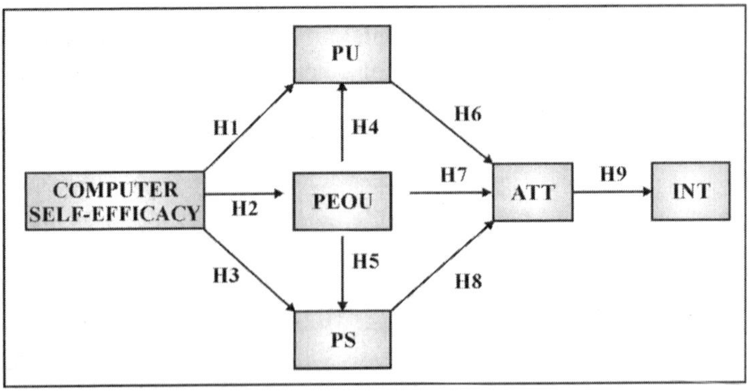

Figure 10 : The research model and hypotheses.

Computer Self-Efficacy

One important factor that influences the adoption of internet banking is the computer and internet proficiency of the consumer.

Consumers need to be familiar with computers in general, and should be, to some extent, proficient in the use of web browsers, to engage in computer-mediated communications and transactions. Having proficiency in these areas will increase a consumer's likelihood of adopting internet banking. Self-efficacy has been examined by many researchers (Compeau and Higgins, 1995; Compeau *et al,* 1999; Hong *et al,* 2001; Agarwal *et al,* 2000; Johnson and Marakas, 2000; Chau, 2001). Prior research has suggested a positive relationship between experience with computing technology and a variety of outcomes such as an affect towards computers and computer usage (Leym and Gordon, 1989; Harrison and Rainer, 1992; Agarwal and Prasad, 1999). This confirms the critical role that computer self-efficacy plays in understanding individual responses to information technology. Self-efficacy, in this study has been further extended to the use of internet and is measured as a skill level of consumers in using computers and internet.

Perceived Usefulness (PU)

Davis (1989) asserts that the decision to use new technology is determined by the extent to which a person believes that it is cost-effective in providing goods or services compared to the current method. PU is defined as the degree to which a person believes that using a particular technology will enhance his performance. The PU is also an important variable from TAM (Araujo and Araujo, 2003; Noteberg *et al.* 2003; Gefen *at al.,* 2003; Matheison, 1991; Malhotra and Galleta, 1999). PU has been confirmed as an important variable that influences user technology acceptance and therefore has received a great deal of attention from previous researchers.

Perceived Ease of Use

Perceived ease of use refers to the degree to which a person believes that using a particular system would be free of effort. According to TAM, the PEOU is one of the main variables influencing the use of technology. Extensive research over the past years provides evidence of the significant effect of perceived ease of use on usage, either directly or indirectly through its effect on perceived usefulness

(Agarwal and Prasad, 1999; Davis *et al,* 1989; Hu *et al,* 1999; Jackson *et al,* 1997; Venkatesh, 1999, 2000; Venkatesh and Davis, 1996, 2000; Venkatesh and Morris, 2000). IT's that are easy to use will be less threatening to the individual (Moon and Kim, 2001). This implies that perceived ease of use is expected to have a positive influence on users in their interaction with internet banking systems. Therefore, the more the consumer perceives internet banking as easy to use, the more he or she is likely to adopt it.

Perceived Security

Perceived security is a major reservation consumers have about internet banking. Concerns about cyber crime, transaction security and errors in transactions can limit adoption of electronic technologies (Gingrade, 1998; Simms, 1999). Security is the state of being free from dangers like theft or losing money and information (Gefen *et al,* 2003). Consumer concerns about security and privacy have been noted by many experts (Miyazaki and Fernandez, 2001; Gefen *et al.,* 2003; Nissenbaum, 2004). One particular survey by Chung and Paynter (2002) identified consumer fear regarding transaction security as an inhibitor to the adoption of internet banking. Security has also been identified as a key consumer concern in other internet banking adoption studies (Black *et al.,* 2002; Siu and Mou, 2005). Hain *et al.,* (2003) observed that non-internet banking consumers were more concerned about security and privacy issues than internet banking consumers.

Security has been identified as one of the biggest barriers for the uptake of internet banking (Sathye, 1999). Cooper (1997) and Daniel (1999) identified that an important factor affecting the acceptance and adoption of an innovation is the level of security and risk associated with it. Even in countries where internet banking has long been established, one of the most important factors slowing its progress is 'the consumers' concern for security of financial transactions over the internet. Security failure at a particular bank could not only cause large losses for that bank, but could spawn a general lack of reliability in internet banking transactions. Awamleh and Fernandes (2005) revealed that security of internet banking transactions has a significant impact on customer satisfaction in internet banking. Security of internet banking transactions was significant for those using internet banking for more than two years. O'Connell (1996) and Daniel (1999) discovered that security concern is an important factor which affects acceptance and adoption of a new technology or an innovation. The hypotheses for the research model are presented in table one.

Chapterisation

In light of the above findings, the present study is undertaken in Indian context to find out recent trends in e-banking and comparative study of selected Public and Private sector Banks. The Study has been divided in the following chapters along with the details:

CHAPTER – I : Defines About Introduction includes Concept, E-Banking, Difference between Traditional Banking and E-Banking, Aspects of E- Banking, Significance of E-Banking, Impediments of E-Banking, Corrective Measures, Innovative Banking, Limitations of the study.

CHAPTER –II : Review of Literature is about Review of Literature, Review of Bygone Studies, Research Problem, Statement of Problem, Introduction, Technology Acceptance Model, The Research Framework, Computer Self-Efficacy, Perceived Usefulness (PU), Perceived Ease of Use, Perceived Security, Chapterisation.

CHAPTER – III : Research Methodology throws light on rationale of the study, Scope of the study, Identification of Problem, Statement of Problem, Importance of Study, Objectives of Research Study, Research Problem, Research Gap, Research Design, Sample Design, Source of Data Collection, Research Tools, Limitations of Study.

Chapter – IV : Profile and E-Banking Services of PNB shows Introduction, Financial Inclusion, Small and Medium Enterprises, E-Banking Initiatives, Recent Awards, Different Schemes of PNB, E-Banking Services in PNB, References.

Chapter - V: Profile and E-Banking Services of SBI expresses about Introduction, Central Banking Function, Specific Purpose,

Human Resource Planning in SBI, E-banking Concept, Internet Banking System, Value Added Services, Products and Services, SBI E-Tax, Fund Transfer.

Chapter - VI: Profile and E-Banking Services of HDFC throws light on HDFC Profile, Progress of HDFC Bank, E-Banking in HDFC, Individual, Benefits of an HDFC Individual Deposit, Housing Finance Sector, Transactional, Banking Services of HDFC Bank, Features and Benefits, Customised Investment Solutions, Investment Options, Wealth Management Programme, E-Broking, Relationship Pricing, Annual Service Charge Waiver, E- Banking in HDFC, Registration for Net Banking of HDFC.

Chapter - VII : Profile and E-Banking Services of ICICI expresses about Bank Profile, History of ICICI Bank, Products and Services Offered by Bank, E-Banking Services in ICICI, Terms and Conditions of Net Banking, Comparison of ICICI and HDFC E-Banking Services.

Chapter - VIII: Data Analysis and Interpretation expresses about Comparative Study of Performance of Selected Banks, Tool and Techniques of Analysis and Period of Study, Camel Technique, Assets Quality, Management Efficiency, Earnings Quality, Liquidity, Overall Ranking, Concept, Anova, Analysis and Interpretation.

Chapter – IX : Conclusion, Observation and Recommendation express about summary and conclusion of the research study, Suggestions and Recommendations of the Study, Limitations, Contribution of the Study, Further Scope of the Study.

REFERENCES

1. Altman, E., Avery, R., Eisenbeis, R., and Sinkey, J. (2000), Application of Classification Techniques in Business Banking and Finance, Connecticut, Connecticut.
2. Baruch, L. (2000), *Financial Statement Analysis: A New Approach*, Prentice Hall, Englewood Cliffs, New Jersey.
3. Bhattacharya, A.; C.A.K. Lovell and Pankaj Sahay (2007), "The Impact of Liberalisation on the Productive Efficiency of Indian Commercial Banks", *European Journal of Operational Research*, Vol. 98, pp. 175-212.

Chapter - III

Research Methodology

Introduction

The word 'research' is derived from the French word 'researcher' which means to seek again. Research is defined as human activity based on intellectual application in the investigation of matter. The primary purpose for applied research is discovering, interpreting, and the development of methods and systems for the advancement of human knowledge on a wide variety of scientific matters of our world and the universe. Research can use the scientific method, but need not do so.

The purpose of this chapter is to present the basic methodology followed to collect data. The detailed discussion around the methodology includes a description of the basic type of research that was conducted, the population and sample, the data collection methods and a brief explanation of the different statistical techniques used to analyse the data. The term research is also used to describe an entire collection of information about a particular subject. According to Kothari (2006), it is the pursuit of trust with the help of study, observation, comparison and experiment.

Research as an activity is directed at "the systematic search for pertinent information on a topic" "Scientific research is systematic, controlled, empirical and critical investigation of hypothetical prepositions about the presumed relations among natural phenomena."

According to Redman & Mory, Research is a "Systematized efforts to gain knowledge."

Research Methodology

Research Methodology is defined as the systematic way of solving any problem. It is a science of studying the scientifically conduction of research. The present research includes all the necessary steps, for the research design in accordance with the requirements of the subject. In the present research it is tried to collect maximum possible information on the subject i.e.

"A CRITICAL STUDY OF TRENDS IN E-BANKING WITH SPECIAL REFERENCE TO SELECTED PUBLIC AND PRIVATE SECTOR BANKS".

The study includes scientific methods, which covers the under-mentioned steps with logic behind each of them.

1. Rationale of the Study
2. Scope of the Study
3. Identification of the Problem
4. Statement of the Problem
5. Importance of the Study
6. Objectives of the Study
7. Research Hypothesis
8. Research Gap
9. Research Design
10. Sample Design
11. Sources of Data
12. Statistical Tools employed for Analysis and Interpretation
13. Analysis and Presentations
14. Limitations of the Study

Rationale of the Study

One has to approach the branch in person, to withdraw cash or deposit a cheque or request a statement of accounts. In true Internet banking, any inquiry or transaction is processed online without any reference to the branch (anywhere banking) at any time. Providing

Internet banking is increasingly becoming a "need to have" than a "nice to have" service. The net banking, thus, now is more of a norm rather than an exception in many developed countries due to the fact that it is the cheapest way of providing banking services.

Scope of the Study

Researcher wants to analyze e-banking data of selected commercial banks. Researcher has selected two banks from private sector and two banks from public sector ICICI Bank and HDFC Bank in Private sector. SBI and PNB in Public sector as a sample for study.

Identification of Problem

In research process, the first and foremost step happens to be that of selecting and properly defining a research problem. The task of defining and identification of research problem, very often, follows a sequential pattern the problem is stated in a general ways, the ambiguities are thinking and rethinking process results is a more specific formulation of the problem. So that it may be a realistic one in forms of available data and resources and it also analytically meaningful.

The problem under study concerns E-Banking in private and public sector banks. It is the corporate philosophy of an organisation about and in relation to its people and it is reflected in its personal policies, and practices and day-to-day decisions affecting the employees. The assumptions of the organisation about human being and their natural, organisation behaviour and organisation itself constitute the under findings of this philosophy.

Truly, speaking the life of human being is more of less influenced by the natural resources, thereby it is influencing the patentability of human beings to discharge their day-to-day functions. And achieve the object of a better and happy life in the present. It is obvious that every individual tries his level best to acquire capability in order to secure job for a better future during his/her life. It is needless to say that the development system of E-Banking is aimed at creating such a climate so that it may be dynamic and growth oriented. It is also a fact that E-Banking services have their unlimited to surface, nurturing and using the capabilities of people in general.

For the purpose of effective functioning of Private and Public Sector banks, it is essential that E-Banking of Private and Public Sector banks should know the facts or requirements to the present working environment in banking sector. Training is only media which can strengthen the ability of a human being to cope with the competitive global challenges of banking sector.

Statement of Problem

With the changing environment, banks implemented tele-banking, mobile banking and call centre services, ATM and others one after another. Due to rapid change in technology and the entry of private and foreign banks a number of new products and delivery channels have been introduced. Among the major initiatives Internet Banking has brought to the customers the much demanded convenience. The advent of internet banking offers banking firms a new frontier of opportunities and challenges. Despite these possibilities, there are various psychological and behavioural issues such as reluctance to change, trust in one's bank, security concerns, preference of human interference and the like impede the growth of internet banking. In this regard a study has been undertaken in Internet banking services provided by the selected Public and Private Sector Banks.

Importance of Study

The banks are now marching towards business diversification. Some of the banks are already engaged in the activities like mutual funds, housing finance, leasing, merchant banking, credit cards and factoring etc. There is pressing need to develop expertise and skill for such activities. Over the last few years, banking as an industry has undergone certain perceptible changes which call for increased emphasis on this important component of E-Banking policy.

With the increasing quantum of deposits advances number of accounts, transactions and other activities, seems no option but to quicken computerisation and banking industry the training system in banking will have to develop expertise and skill for effective utilisation of these modern tools. There is a need to prepare and train staff at branches abroad in such a way that they may compete with the most well organised international banks.

As far as banks executives are concerned the training will have to play a vital role because in the changed environment, confidence and leadership quality has to be developed among executives.

The main focus of training will have to be on inculcation of ability for tackling uncertainties, understanding people, technology and system of environment nationally and internationally as also on building a good team.

Objectives of Study

1. To discover the basic relationship which may lead to improve E-Banking Services in such areas as recruitment, selection, training, promotion, performance appraisal, transfer, absenteeism, discipline grievances, job satisfaction, trade union and relation in the selected banks.
2. To evaluate the effect and results of current policies, E-Banking programmes and practice in the selected banks.
3. To know the functions of management in mobilising of E-Banking in PNB, SBI, ICICI and HDFC Bank.
4. To collect information about employee's attitude regarding E-Banking services in selected banks.
5. To extent my knowledge and undertaking in E-Banking.
6. To have a practical knowledge in the Research.
7. E-Banking is concerned with environment.
8. It is concerned with personal policies.
9. It is of a continuous in nature and cordial with environment.
10. It ensures economic, social and individual satisfaction.
11. It is part of total management of an organisation.
12. To evaluate effectiveness of E-Banking programme by assessing the quality of output and productivity.

13. To provide an opportunity and comprehensive framework for the development of E-Banking services in an organisation for full expansions of their latent and manifest potential.
14. To maximize the utilisation of E-Banking and Human Resource for the achievement of individual and organisation goal.
15. To analyze the change in the attitude or behaviour through training.
16. To analyze the role of training institute in promoting importance of training at PNB, SBI, ICICI and HDFC.
17. To ascertain the perception of customers regarding the service quality of banks.
18. To analyse and compare the perception of the customers about Public Sector Banks and Private Sector Banks.
19. To examine the impact of perception of service quality on the customers satisfaction.
20. To identify the discriminating factors of service quality among the two group of banks.

Research Hypotheses

In simple words hypotheses means a mere assumption or some supposition to be proved or disproved. A research hypothesis is a predictive statement, capable of being tested by scientific methods, that relates an independent variable to some dependent variable. So hypothesis is the first and vital step of the research and it is also known as the principal instrument in research.

E-Banking principles and practices are better in Public Sector Banks than in Private Sector Banks. The present study is to analyze a few aspects of E-Banking in selected banks. Good methodology is the life blood of any research work. The source of any research work largely depends upon correct selective and application of the most suitable method in accordance with volume of information to be covered in the proposed shed. In order to achieve effectiveness of study both primary and secondary sources of data will be used.

Hypothesis of the present study are:

- E-Banking programmes of the Private Sector Banks and Public Sector Banks have been able to achieve their aims and objective.
- E-Banking function in Private Sector Banks and Public Sector Banks have been able to improve performance of the employees.
- There is visible difference among those who have undergone training in terms of skills.
- Selected Private Sector and Public Sector Banks have been able to receive substantial impact on training investment.
- E-Banking of Public Sector Banks is better than Private Sector Banks.

Research Gap

The review of literature suggest that most of the studies have been done on issues related to Internet banking in countries like Australia (Sathye, 1999), Malaysia (Mukti, 2000; Chung and Paynter, 2002; Sohail and Shanmugham, 2004), Singapore (Gerrard and Cunningham, 2003a, 2006b), Turkey vs. UK (Sayar and Wolfe, 2007) and Saudi Arabia (Sohail and Shaikh, 2007). Much work has not been done in India with regard to Internet banking issues. The present study intends to know the factors affecting the acceptance of e-banking by the customers and also indicates level of concern regarding security and privacy issues in Indian context.

As per the review of few literatures above, it becomes clear that after liberalisation banking sector in India has shown a remarkable progress, mainly by the new private sector banks and foreign banks. Public sector banks are also coming in the competition with them. Performances of public sector banks are not very efficient, but will soon show some good progress in the coming years. Banking in India is not limited to deposits and withdrawal but introducing many new services and products. Today's banks are now more customers oriented. So this research study is helpful to increase the efficiency of human resource through E-Banking programmes in banks.

Research Design

A research design is the arrangement of conditions for collection and analyses of data in a manner that aims to combine relevance to the research purpose with economy in procedure. In fact, the research design is the conceptual structure within research is conducted, it constituted the blueprint for the collection, measurement and analysis of data.

Research design in the present study is of descriptive nature to analysis the performance of training in bank with the help of data collected from various source. The study falls under the category of descriptive and diagnostic research study. This type of research is concerned with specific predictions, with narration of facts and characteristics concerning individuals, group or situation. Descriptive research studies are those studies which are concerned with describing the characteristics of a particular individual, or of a group, whereas diagnostic research studies determine the frequency with which something occurs or its association with something else. The research design in such type of study must make enough provision for protection against bias and must maximize reliability, with due concern for the economical completion of the research study.

Sample Design

A sample design is a definite plan for obtaining a sample from a given population. It refers to the technique or the procedure the researcher would adopt in selecting items for the sample. Sample design may as well lay down the number of items to be included in the sample i.e. size of the sample about E-Banking services of ICICI, HDFC, PNB and SBI Banks. 153 employees and 20 HR manager or general managers of the Private Sector Banks and Public Sector Banks associated with different training institutes are approached. Simple Random Sampling or probability sampling technique is used to select the sample. Under this sampling design, every item of the universe has an equal chance of inclusion in the sample under random sampling. Cluster and Area sampling technique is preferred.

Source of Data

There can be two methods of generating information or collecting data required for research, one through observation and the other through experimentation. Observation is the process of measuring variables just as they occur in nature, without directly or deliberately influencing their value. Experimentation method has the foundation of science. Its essence is the process of manipulating an independent variable and then measuring the resulting change in the dependent variable.

The required data have been taken from annual reports of the selected banks and other publications. It is expected that present study will not only be useful to management of these banks but also to customer, social, scientist, share holding employed country development as a whole. It includes study of E-Banking in selected banks from April 2008 to March 2013.

The data is collected through primary and secondary sources.

Primary data: The primary data, which is essential for investigation and statistical analysis, was collected through:

(a) Structured questionnaire tool

A questionnaire is a set of questions arranged logically, divided into sections and groups, drawn with the object of collecting information about various aspects of the subject of research. The questionnaire is designed keeping in view the object, scope, subject matter and other aspects of the research problem. Quite often, questionnaire is considered as the heart of a survey operation. Hence, it should be very carefully constructed. If it is not properly set up then the survey is bound to fail.

(b) Formal interviews with the human resource department managers and general managers of different branches of selected banks.

On the basis of the impressions gained through the objective analysis of different types of primary and secondary data, interviews may be arranged with key functionaries in a given area. The use of this technique needs a certain degree of appreciation of empirical investigation and requires a sound awareness of organisational dynamics.

(c) Informal interviews, discussions and interactions with relevant persons in the field of training and development, trainees and training institutions.

Secondary data - Secondary data are available readymade as collected by other. The researcher has undertaken review of published literature relating to training facilities available in the banks. For this research secondary data were obtained from:

- Annual Reports of ICICI, HDFC, PNB and SBI.
- Reports on working of training division of ICICI, HDFC, PNB and SBI.
- Research Methodology 58
- Reports of various committees on training in E-Banking services.
- Proceedings of various conferences and seminars on training.
- Journals, Books, magazines, newspapers.
- Reports prepared by research scholars.
- Internet has been the pool of information during whole period. Maximum data was collected through this source.

STATISTICAL TOOLS EMPLOYED FOR ANALYSIS AND INTERPRETATION

In the present study, researcher has selected four banks two public sector banks and two private sector banks. Four banks namely PNB, SBI, ICICI and HDFC. Present study is mainly based on secondary data. The relevant data, in this regard is collected from PROCESS Data base of CMIE (Center for Monitoring Indian Economy).

For the purpose of research researcher has used a CAMEL technique for E-Banking analysis of selected banks. The period of study for E-Banking in present study is taken 5 years from 2008-09 to 2013-14. Researcher has used simple statistical measures like mean and standard deviation. For testing hypothesis researcher has used F test.

1. **CAMEL APPROACH**

Camel is a technique of ratio analysis which covers five category ratios of banks.

CAMEL stands for

- **C-Capital Adequacy**

  Capital Adequacy means to Risk-Weighted Assests. A sound capital base strengthens confidence of depositors.

- **A-Asset Quality**

  Non-performing loans to total loans indicative a quality of banking credit decision. Higher GNPA is indicative of poor decision making.

- **M-Management**

  Non-interest expenditures to total assests measures working of the management. Expensive such as payroll, workers compensation and training investment reflect the management policy stance.

- **E-Earning Quality**

  All income from operations, non-traditional sources, extra ordinary items. It can be measured as the return on assest ratio.

- **L -Liquidity**

  Cash maintained by the banks and balances with the central bank, to total asset ratio is an indicator of banks liquidity.

2. **PERCENTAGE (%) METHOD**

Percentages are often used in data presentation for they simplify numbers reducing all of them to a 0 to 100 range. Through the use of percentages, the data are reduced in the standard form with base equal to 100 which fact facilitates relative comparisons.

3. **MEASURES OF CENTRAL TENDENCY**

Measures of Central Tendency (or statistical averages) tell us the point about which items have a tendency to cluster. Such a measure is considered as the most representative figure for the entire mass of data. Measure of Central Tendency is also known as statistical average. Mean, Median and Mode are the most popular averages. Mean also known as arithmetic average, is the most common measure of central tendency and may be defined as the value, which we get by dividing the total of the values of various given items in a series by the total number of items. It is the simplest measurement of central tendency and is a widely used measure. Its chief use consists in summarising the essential features of a series and in enabling data to be compared.

It will help in representation of graphs. It will help in determining the average number of people/respondents falling in category favouring particular attribute.

4. **F-TEST**

R. A Fisher J developed the technique of F-test. F-test is generally known as the variance ratio test and is mostly used in the context of analysis of variance.

$$F=\frac{\sigma^2 1}{c^2 2}$$

5. **ANNOVA TEST**

The Annova Test is the initial step in identifying factors that are influencing a given data set. After the Annova test is performed, the analyst is able to perform further analysis on the systematic factors that are systematically contributing to the data set's variability.

Analysis and Presentations

The process of selecting a data analysis strategy is one of the fundamentals on which the outcome of whole research depends. Analysis in relation to statistical data involves estimation of the values of unknown parameters of population, testing the hypothesis and drawing inferences there from. A statistics is a quantitative characteristic of a sample and a parameter is a quantitative characteristic of a population. Data Analysis is not end in itself. Its purpose is to produce information that will help in address the problem.

There are several techniques which may be appropriate for analyzing the data for a given project or research problem. The present study has taken into account all such matters and done analysis and presentations with the help of standardized techniques.

Limitations of Study

Since this study involves collection of primary data using structured questionnaire supported with personal interest all our efforts were made to check, reduce and minimized ambiguous responses as provided by the selected respondents' bank employees that may lead to distorted and incorrect data information, analysis and findings.

It would be appropriate to put forward limitations to the study as follows:

1. The respondents are drawn solely from urban population only; hence it would be in appropriate to generalise it as fit and good for the whole of the population.
2. Sometimes behaviour of the respondent was not good towards researcher.
3. In some branches employees were not willing to give any information regarding the working of the bank.
4. The answers of some questions were not correct and it leads to create a problem while accessing the data.

While conducting the study every effort made to conduct the study as rigorously as possible, certain limitations were however unavoidable. The present research may have some limitation as follows:

- There is a possibility that respondents interpret a question differently as per his understanding and interpretations.

commencement of Pakistani independence, PNB lost its premises in Lahore, but continued to operate in Pakistan. PNB had already shifted its registered office from Lahore to Calcutta in June 1947 — even before the announcement of the Partition. 1951: PNB acquired the 39 branches of Bharat Bank (est. 1942); Bharat Bank became Bharat Nidhi Ltd. 1960: PNB again shifted its head office, this time from Calcutta to Delhi. 1961: PNB acquired Universal Bank of India. 1963: The Government of Burma nationalised PNB's branch in Rangoon (Yangon). September 1965: After the Indo-Pak war the government of Pakistan seized all the offices in Pakistan of Indian banks. PNB also had one or more branches in East Pakistan (Bangladesh). 1960s: PNB amalgamated Indo Commercial Bank (est. 1933) in a rescue. 1969: The Government of India (GOI) nationalised PNB and 13 other major commercial banks, on 19 July 1969. 1976 or 1978: PNB opened a branch in London. 1986: The Reserve Bank of India required PNB to transfer its London branch to State Bank of India after the branch was involved in a fraud scandal. 1986: PNB acquired Hindustan Commercial Bank (est. 1943) in a rescue. The acquisition added Hindustan's 142 branches to PNB's network. 1993: PNB acquired New Bank of India, which the GOI had nationalised in 1980. 1998: PNB set up a representative office in Almaty, Kazakhstan. 2003: PNB took over Nedungadi Bank, the oldest private sector bank in Kerala. At the time of the merger with PNB, Nedungadi Bank's shares had zero value, with the result that its shareholders received no payment for their shares.

PNB also opened a representative office in London. 2004: PNB established a branch in Kabul, Afghanistan. PNB also opened a representative office in Shanghai. PNB established an alliance with Everest Bank in Nepal that permits migrants to transfer funds easily between India and Everest Bank's 12 branches in Nepal. 2005: PNB opened a representative office in Dubai. 2007: PNB established PNBIL – Punjab National Bank (International) – in the UK, with two offices, one in London, and one in South Hall. Since then it has opened a third branch in Leicester, and is planning a fourth in Birmingham. 2008: PNB opened a branch in Hong Kong. 2009: PNB opened a representative office in Oslo, Norway, and a second branch in Hong Kong, this in Kowloon. 2010: PNB received permission to upgrade its representative office in the Dubai International Financial Centre to a branch.

PNB was founded in the year 1895 at Lahore (presently in Pakistan) as an offshoot of the Swadeshi Movement. Among the inspired founders were Sardar Dayal Singh Majithia, Lala Har Kishen Lal, Lala Lalchand, Shri Kali Prosanna Roy, Shri E.C. Jessawala, Shri Prabhu Dayal, Bakshi Jaishi Ram, Lala Dholan Dass. With a common missionary zeal they set about establishing a national bank; the first one with Indian capital — owned, managed and operated by the Indians for the benefit of the Indians. The Lion of Punjab, Lala Lajpat Rai, was actively associated with the management of the Bank in its formative years. The Bank made steady progress right from its inception. It has shown resilience to tide over many a crisis. It withstood the crisis in banking industry of 1913 and the severe depression of the thirties.

It survived the most critical period in its history - the Partition of 1947 - when it was uprooted from its major area of operations. It was the farsightedness of the management that the registered office of the Bank was shifted from Lahore to Delhi in June 1947 - even before the announcement of the Partition. With the passage of time the Bank grew to strength spreading its wings from one corner of the country to another. Some smaller banks like, The Bhagwan Dass Bank Limited, Universal Bank of India, The Bharat Bank Limited, The Indo-Commercial Bank Limited, The Hindustan Commercial Bank Limited and The Nedungadi Bank were brought within its fold.

PNB has the privilege of maintaining accounts of the illustrious national leaders like Mahatma Gandhi, Shri Jawahar Lal Nehru, Shri Lal Bahadur Shastri, Shrimati Indira Gandhi besides the account of the famous Jalianwala Bagh Committee.

Nationalisation of the fourteen major banks on 19th July, 1969 was a major step for the banking industry. PNB was one amongst these. As a result, banking was given a new direction and thrust. The banks were expected to reach people in every nook and corner, meet their needs, and work for their economic upliftment. Removal of poverty and regional imbalances were accorded a high priority.

PNB has always responded enthusiastically to the nation's needs. It has been earnestly engaged in the task of national development. In the process, the bank has emerged as a major nationalised bank. With over 60 million satisfied customers and more than 5100 offices including 5 overseas branches, PNB has continued to retain its leadership position amongst the nationalised banks. The bank enjoys strong fundamentals, large franchise value and good brand image. Besides being ranked as one of India's top service brands, PNB has remained fully committed to its guiding principles of sound and prudent banking. Apart from offering banking products, the bank has also entered the credit card, debit card; bullion business; life and non-life insurance; Gold coins and asset management business, etc. PNB has earned many awards and accolades during the year in appreciation of excellence in services, Corporate Social Responsibility (CSR) practices, transparent governance structure, best use of technology and good human resource management.

Since its humble beginning in 1895 with the distinction of being the first Swadeshi Bank to have been started with Indian capital, PNB has achieved significant growth in business which at the end of March 2011 amounted to Rs 5,55,005 crore. PNB is ranked as the 2nd largest bank in the country after SBI in terms of branch network, business and many other parameters. During the FY 2010-11, with 39.16% share of CASA to domestic deposits, the Bank achieved a net profit of Rs 4433 crore. Bank has a strong capital base with capital adequacy ratio of 12.42% as on Mar '11 as per Basel II with Tier I and Tier II capital ratio at 8.44% and 3.98% respectively. As on March '11, the Bank has the Gross and Net NPA ratio of 1.79% and 0.85% respectively. During the FY 2010-11, its ratio of Priority Sector Credit to Adjusted Net Bank Credit at 40.67% and Agriculture Credit to Adjusted Net Bank Credit at 19.30% was also higher than the stipulated requirement of 40% and 18% respectively.

The Bank has been able to maintain its stakeholders' interest by posting an improved NIM of 3.96% in Mar '11 (3.57% Mar '10). The Earning per Share improved to Rs 140.60 (Rs 123.86 Mar '10) while the Book value per share improved to Rs 661.20 (Rs 514.77 Mar '10). Punjab National Bank continues to maintain its frontline position in the Indian banking industry. In particular, the bank has retained its NUMBER ONE position among the nationalised banks in terms of number of branches, Deposit, Advances, total Business, Assets, Operating and Net profit in the year 2010-11. The impressive operational and financial performance has been brought about by Bank's focus on customer based business with thrust on CASA deposits, Retail, SME and Agri Advances and with more inclusive approach to banking; better asset liability management; improved margin management, thrust on recovery and increased efficiency in core operations of the Bank.

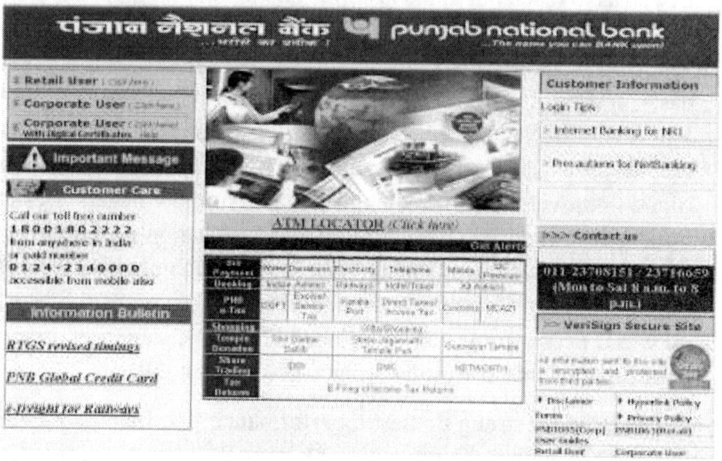

Figure 11 : E-Banking Services of PNB.

E-Banking Services of PNB

Bank always looked at technology as a key facilitator to provide better customer service and ensured that its 'IT strategy' follows the 'Business strategy' so as to arrive at "Best Fit". The Bank has made rapid strides in this direction. All branches of the Bank are under Core Banking Solution (CBS) since Dec '08, thus covering 100% of its business and providing 'Anytime Anywhere' banking facility to all customers including customers of more than 3200 rural and semi urban branches. The Bank has also been offering Internet banking services to its customers which also enables on line booking of rail tickets, payment of utilities bills, purchase of airline tickets, etc. Towards developing a cost effective alternative channels of delivery, the Bank with 5050 ATMs has the largest ATM network amongst Nationalised Banks.

With the help of advanced technology, the Bank has been a front runner in the industry so far as the initiatives for Financial Inclusion is concerned. With its policy of inclusive growth, the Bank's mission is "Banking for Unbanked". The Bank has launched a drive for biometric smart card based technology enabled Financial Inclusion with the help of Business Correspondents/ Business Facilitators (BC/ BF) so as to reach out to the last mile customer. The Bank has started several innovative initiatives for marginal groups like rickshaw pullers, vegetable vendors, dairy farmers, construction workers, etc. Bank has launched a welfare scheme of adoption of village viz., "PNB VIKAS". Under the scheme, Bank has selected 117 villages (60 in lead districts and 57 in non-lead district) in different circles for all-round improvement in the living standards of the villagers. Besides, Bank has formed "PNB PRERNA", an association of the wives of the Bank's senior management. The association through its voluntary initiatives has undertaken activities like distribution of food to the poor and needy, provision of computers, books, stationary items to poor girl students at various orphanages and schools etc.

Backed by strong domestic performance, the Bank is planning to realise its global aspirations. Bank has opened one branch each at Kabul and Dubai, two branches at Hong Kong and an Offshore Banking Unit at Mumbai. In addition to the above, Bank has Representative offices at Almaty, Dubai, Shanghai and Oslo, a wholly owned subsidiary in UK with seven branches and a subsidiary each in Kazakhstan & Bhutan, and joint venture with Everest Bank Ltd. Nepal. During the year, Bank acquired majority equity stake of 63.64% in Dana Bank of Kazakhstan.

Punjab National Bank (PNB) is one of the largest bank having 500 branches in the world, and enjoys a rich history and heritage. PNB was the first Indian bank to be started solely with Indian capital. Established in 1895 at Lahore, and nationalised in 1969, it has worked assiduously to build the banking sector in rural and urban India.

It has presence in remote areas of the country, cutting across cultural and linguistic boundaries.

PNB's principal activities are to provide treasury and banking operations. The activities include accepting deposits, lending loans and to provide other financial related services. The banking operations provides short and long term loans to agricultural, small scale industries and other priority sectors. PNB also offers internet banking facilities to its customers. PNB is 100% CBS and operates through 4869 branches, 444 extension counters and 1855 ATMs.

- Bank has recently opened its branch in Duabi International Financial Centre (DIFC), Dubai, United Arab Emirates. The branch has started functioning after its soft launch on 20th December, 2009 with a Category I license.
- PNB is shortly going to start operations of its joint venture subsidiary Druk PNB Bank Ltd in Bhutan.
- Bank is also pursuing upgradation of its presence in China and Norway besides, seeking a presence in Australia.
- Bank is in the process of setting up:-
  - A joint venture subsidiary at Kazakhstan by acquiring a 63.64% stake with management control in Dana Bank of Kazakhstan. Agreements have been finalised with Financial Market Supervision Agency.
  - A wholly owned subsidiary at Canada for which approval of the Canadian regulator OSFI (Office of Superintendent of Financial Institution) is awaited.

Financial Inclusion

- Under Branchless banking model of financial inclusion, the bank is implementing 47 projects in 17 States. Out of these, 39 are technology based financial inclusion projects while other 8 are credit driven projects.
- The bank has launched an ambitious 'Project Namaskar' under which 1 lakh touch points will be established in unbanked villages by 2013 to extend the bank's outreach and create a large customer base.

Small and Medium Enterprises

- SME Centres (HUB) has been set up at Delhi, Kolkata, Chennai, Mumbai, Ludhiana, Amritsar and Chandigarh.
- Bank's Rehabilitation/Care Centers at Circle Offices/SME branches are manned by experienced officials to guide the MSME units on their financial needs and the facilities available from the banks/Govt/RBI.
- Implemented the 'Scoring Models' for SME advances upto Rs 2 crore.

E-Banking Initiatives

Under PNB Krishak Saathi (Debt Swap Scheme), the Bank has financed Rs 139.75 crore to 34,459 farmers upto Dec 2009 for repaying the debt taken from private money lenders.

- During the 9 months of 2009-10, the Bank conducted 4894 Kisan Gosthies wherein 1.97 lakh farmers benefitted through marketing dissemination of useful information.
- Bank has operationalised 8 Farmers' Training Centres where more than 46,000 persons have been trained during Apr-Dec 2009 at Bank's cost including around 9500 women.
- Around 15,000 animals have been treated at the Animal check-up camps organised by the Bank and around 6000 persons have been provided free medical advice.
- PNB is the first nationalised bank to implement an Enterprise-wide Data warehouse to integrate Data from multiple source systems and provides MIS and data feed to Anti Money Laundering and Operational Risk Solution. Operational Risk Solution has been operationalised to monitor compliance with BASEL II requirements.
- ECS (Electronic Clearing System) facility has been provided in 981 branches of the Bank at 49 Centres.
- Of the 6 PNB Sponsored RRBs, 3 RRBs branches have become 100% CBS. Out of 1389 branches in, 719 branches have been migrated to CBS.

- Impressive response to bank's 'CASA Campaign' during August-Dec, 2009, more than 16 lakh CASA accounts were opened.
- To facilitate factoring, forfeiting and trade finance related business, a joint venture company namely M/s India Factoring and Finance Solutions Pvt. Ltd. has been incorporated in Dec '09 in collaboration with FIM Bank (Malta), Banca IFIS (Italy) and Blend Financial Service with our stake being 30%.
- The Festival Bonanza continues for housing and Car loans till Jan 31, 2010 with rebate in interest rates and processing fees.

Recent Awards

- Golden Peacock Innovative Product/Service Award 2010 presented by Institute of Directors.
- Social and Corporate Governance Award under the category of "Best Corporate Social Responsibility Practice" 2010 awarded by Bombay Stock Exchange.
- Corporate Governance: Golden Peacock Award for Excellence in Corporate Governance (2009) presented by Institute of Directors.
- India Pride Awards for excellence in PSU (2009) presented by Dainik Bhaskar in association with Daily News and Analysis.
- IT 3 Awards – CIO 100 Awards (2009); Emerson Uptime Champion Award and IBM information on Demand (2009).
- SME: 2 Awards for excellent performance in lending under Prime Minister's Employment Generation Programme (PMEGP); 3 Awards for excellence in institutional finance in propagating KVIC programmes.
- Best Employer Brand Award under the Regional Round Award Winners-Indore at 4th Employer branding Awards 2009-10 presented by Employer Branding institute, India.

Different Schemes Provided by Punjab National Bank

Savings Fund Account

- PNB Premium Saving Account
- PNB Prudent Sweep
- Total Freedom Salary Account
- High End Salary Account
- Family Suraksha Bachat Khata
- PNB Junior SF Account
- PNB Vidyarthi SF Account
- Basic Saving Bank Deposit Account (BSBDA)
- PNB Rakshak Scheme
- PNB Shikshak Sweep Scheme
- PNB Shikshak Overdraft Scheme
- Scheme for Providing Overdraft Facility to Pensioners

Current Account

- PNB Smart Banking Current Account
- PNB Current Account

Fixed Deposit Schemes

- Auto renewal
- E-FD
- FD Scheme for Road Accident Victims
- Recurring Deposit Scheme
- Penalty Clause For Pre-Mature Cancellation/Part Withdrawal of Domestic Term Deposit
- PNB Anupam Term Deposit Scheme
- PNB Balika Shiksha
- PNB Capital Gain Account Scheme
- PNB Dugna Deposit Scheme
- PNB Lakhpati Deposit Scheme-A

- PNB Lakhpati Deposit Scheme (Recurring and Fixed Deposit)-B
- PNB Multi Benefit Term Deposit Scheme
- PNB Saksham
- PNB Scheme for Road Accident Victims
- PNB Special Recurring Deposit Product
- PNB Special Term Deposit Scheme
- PNB Sugam Term Deposit Scheme
- PNB Swechha Jama Yojna/Flexi RD
- PNB Ordinary Term Deposit Scheme
- PNB Varshik Aay Yojana (VAY) Deposit Scheme
- PNB Tax Saver Fixed Deposit Scheme
- Prospective Sr. Citizen Scheme
- Loan against Term Deposits
- Terms and Conditions for Joint Term Deposit Accounts

Credit Schemes

- Check List
- List of Retail Asset Branches
- Time schedule for disposal of Retails Loan Applications
- Housing Loan [PNB Flexible Housing Loan] — "Private Builder's Approved Project on PAN India Basis"
- Car Finance - "Retail Tie-Up"
- Two Wheeler Finance
- Personal Loan
- Professional Loan
- Concessional Education Loans to Persons with Disabilities (PwDs)
- PNB Festival Season Bonanza Offer 2014-15
- PNB Saraswati – for Pursuing Higher Studies in India and Abroad
- PNB Kamgaar - for Pursuing Vocational/ Skill Development Courses

- PNB Pratibha - Education Loan Scheme for 103 premier institutes
- Concessional Education Loan to Persons with Disabilities (PwDs)
- Loan Against Mortgage of Property
- Personal Loan Scheme for Pensioners
- Reverse Mortgage Scheme
- Other Credit Scheme
- Advance against Gold and Jewellery

E-Banking Services of Punjab National Bank

1. **Internet Banking:-** Internet Banking System is an electronic medium to bank on line in your account. It is free, safe, faster, convenient and can be used any time. Internet Banking System is one of the fastest most convenient way to access your account, view balances, transfer funds and pay your bill online. You can perform banking transaction online whenever and wherever you want safely from any PC with internet access.
2. **Mobile Banking:-** The esteemed customers of PNB can avail to mobile banking facilities. The Bank makes a commitment in leveraging the latest and emerging trend to serve the customers better and faster. The Mobile banking services comprise best of the security features. The bank promises to establish a standard in banking in out long relationships as they believe their success is based on the satisfaction of the customers.

   Security Features:-

   - Separate password would be provided for login and transaction.
   - The system stores the password in an encryption of one way in database.
   - The user ID gets disabled if the customers does not avail to the services for more than 180 days.

- The password must be changed during login for the Ist time.
- The system focus the user to change the ID and password after the expiry period.
- The login ID is disabled after five consecutive unsuccessful login attempts.

3. **ASBA:- "ASBA means Application Supported By Blocked Amount".** ASBA is an application containing an authorisation to block the application money in the bank account for subscribing to an issue. If an investor is applying through ASBA his application money shall be debited from the bank account only if his / her application is selected for allotment, after the basis of allotment is finalised or the issue is withdrawn/failed.
4. **Share Trading:-** Online trading is offering from PNB which has been made possible by PNB joining hands with SMC. This would be actually a three in one account comprising of:-
   - PNB Bank Account
   - PNB Demat Account
   - SMC Online Trading Account

   All the three accounts have been integrated with each other to offer a hassle free and convenient trading experience to the customer. In case of buying the funds would get debited from the savings account and similarly in case of selling shares from Demat Account without any physical writing of cheque or Demat slip.
5. **E-Tax Payment:-** PNB renders its customers the facility to pay service tax and excise duty online. This can be availed by customer of any core banking branches of the bank. For using this facility the customers must be get registered with the department of central excise and custom as assesses for either central excise or service tax. Also the customers should have an internet banking ID.

6. **Money Transfer:-** For facilitating remittances from across the globe, PNB has tie up for money transfer service western union with Weizmann Forex Ltd. for collecting remittances with a ceiling of USD 2500 on individual remittance. The service is fast, convenient and secured to remit money to PNB.
7. **PNB Global Credit Card:-** PNB Global credit card are issued for domestic usage unless specifically requested for enabling the card for international usage. Your PNB Global credit card can be used world wide. You can use your card for the following:-
   - For Making Purchases
   - For Cash Withdrawal
   - For E-commerce Transaction
   - For Bill Payments

Questionnaire Regarding Process of E-Banking in PNB

1. How do I get register to Internet Banking Services?
2. But I do not have an account with PNB?
3. How do I get password for the Internet Banking Services?
4. I am a NRI customer, can I use Internet Banking?
5. I am not in India, how do I apply for Internet Banking Services?
6. Why are the Passwords so cryptic?
7. What is my user-id for IBS?
8. Within how many days will I get my password?

1. **How do I get register to Internet Banking Services?**

   The Retail customers having account in single name (Self operated account) with debit card facility may register for PNB Internet Banking Services online at our website www.netpnb.com or at any PNB ATM.

   Other eligible customers may get registered for the Internet Banking Services with the branch by filling request form or by recording their request at bank's call centre.

2. But I do not have an account with PNB?

The Internet Banking Service is available to PNB customers only. We shall be glad to accept you as PNB customer and have your account with us. Walk in to any of our branches for opening of account with us and availing Internet Banking Services.

3. How do I get password for the Internet Banking Services?

If you opt for online registration facility, you will have to set your passwords online.

If you register for Internet Banking at PNB ATM, you have the option to get your Passwords delivered at your base branch or at your registered address. After getting the passwords, kindly get it enabled from the branch.

If you register through call centre, you have the option to get your Passwords delivered at any PNB branch or at your registered address. After getting the passwords, kindly get it enabled from the branch.

If you have submitted request for Internet Banking Services in the branch, you will get your Password from the same branch. While collecting password from the branch, please submit the acknowledgement letter duly signed in the branch.

4. I am a NRI customer, can I use Internet Banking?

Yes, NRI customers can use Internet Banking.

5. I am not in India, how do I apply for Internet Banking Services?

If you want to register for Internet Banking, when you are outside India.

1. Download the request form from Internet Banking website and fill the same.
2. Submit your request form with a copy of your passport to the branch where you have account(s).

6. Why are the Passwords so cryptic?

The passwords are generated randomly by the system, which is fully automated and have its own process of using the alpha, numeric and special characters. These passwords are required once only on first access and need to be changed by the customer mandatory for further access. These are in encrypted form in the system and are not known to Bank.

7. What is my user-id for IBS?

If you are Retail IBS User, the Customer Id in PNB will be your user Id for Internet Banking after enabling your account for this facility.

The Customer Id is also mentioned in the 2nd page of your account pass book. You can also ask your branch for the Customer Id / IBS user id.

8. Within how many days will I get my password?

You can expect the password to reach the branch within 6 working days after giving request at the branch. An SMS is also sent to this effect on registered mobile number. In case of online registration, you will have to set the passwords yourself.

STEPS FOR ONLINE REGISTRATION FOR INTERNET BANKING SERVICE THROUGH INTERNET IN PUNJAB NATIONAL BANK BY THE A/C HOLDER HAVING ATM / DEBIT CARD

1. Visit http://netpnb.com and click on "Register here" button caption, given below login button.
2. Go to the end of page and click on "Agree" button.
3. Enter your a/c no and Date of birth or PAN card no. and choose type of facility "View & Transaction" Now, click "Submit" button.
4. Click on "Generate OTP" button.
   (a) SMS of One Time Password (OTP) will be received on your registered mobile.
   (b) Now fill OTP received as SMS in your Mobile into Enter "generated OTP" box.

   Now, click "Submit OTP" button.

5. Enter your Debit/ATM card no. and Debit/ATM card PIN in respective boxes.

   Now, click on "Submit" button.

6. Enter your login password of your choice of minimum 08 characters consisting minimum 01 special character (like *or # or @) and then re-enter same login password.

   (a) In the same way Enter your transaction password (different from Login Password) of your choice of 08 characters consisting minimum 01 special character (like *or # or @) and then re-enter same transaction password.

   (b) Now click on "Register" button.

7. System will display the process completion message and your IBS facility will be activated within 24-48 Hrs of successful registration.

REFERENCES

1. Agarwal, B.P. (1981). Commercial Banking in Indian after Nationalisation– A study of Their Policies and Progress, Classical Publishing Company, New Delhi.
2. Bhagawati, P. and Agarwal, D. (1981). Commercial Banking in India after nationalisation – A study of Their Policies and Progress. Classical Publishing Company, New Delhi. Vol. 272, p. 22cm. pp. 332.
3. Bhaskar, P.V. (2004). Customer Service in Banks. IBA Bulletin ,Vol. XXVI, No. 8 (August), pp. 9-13
4. Brodeur, M. (1998). Satisfaction, dissatisfaction and complaining behaviour with consumer services and intangible products. Indiana University Graduate School of Business, DBA dissertation
5. Customer Satisfaction a Key Growth to Banks: An Article from 'The Hindu', 7 August, 2006.
6. Customer Satisfaction in Indian Banking: A case study of Yamuna Nagar District in Haryana. Political Economy Journal of India, Jan- June, 2008.
7. Desai, V. (1991). Indian Banking, Nature and Problems, Himalaya Publishing House, Bombay.
8. Hasanbanu, S. (2004). Customer Service in Rural Banks: An Analytical Study of Attitude of Different types of Customers towards Banking Services. IBA Bulletin, Vol. XXVI, No. 8 (August), pp. 21-25.
9. Moutinha, L.,Curry, B. (1994). Consumer perceptions of ATMs: An application of neural network. Journal of Marketing Management, Vol. 10 No. 1, pp. 191-206.

10. Moutinho, L., and Meidan, A. (1989). Bank customers' perceptions innovation and new technology. International Journal of Bank Marketing, Vol.7 No. 2, pp. 22-7.
11. Narasimham. (2008). Efficiency, Productivity and Customer Service in Banks. PNB Monthly Review, February.
12. Parasuraman, A., Zeithaml, A., and Berry L.L. (1988). SERVQUAL: A multi-item scale for measuring consumer perceptions of service quality. Journal of Retailing, Vol. 64(1), 12-40.
13. Report of the Committee on Customer Service in Banks, Goiporia, M.N., R.B.I., December, 2003.
14. Report of the Committee on the Financial System, Narasimham M., November, 2002.

Chapter - V

Profile and E-banking Services of SBI

Introduction

The 'State Bank of India' is the premier commercial bank of India. It is expected to perform all the functions as lead bank of commercial bank in India. The State Bank of India was constituted on July 1, 1955 with the passing of the "State Bank of India Act, 1955" by taking over the entire assets and liabilities of Imperial Bank of India. The Imperial Bank of India was established in 1921 through the amalgamation of the three presidency banks of Madras, Bombay and Bengal. This amalgamation was proposed by these banks themselves to compete the possible danger of some foreign banks in England. The Imperial Bank of India was thus brought into existence on January 27, 1921 by the 'Imperial Bank of India Act of 1920.'

Under the Imperial Bank Act governing body of the Bank was the Central Board. Its functions were defined in bye-laws. There were local boards at three presidency towns with fairly wide powers of managing local business but they were under the control of the Central Board. The Central Board was composed of the President, one of the Vice Presidents of the local Boards representing the share holders, the Controllers of Currency representing the Government of India, four Governors nominated by the Government to serve representation of the interests of the Indian community in general, the Secretaries of local Boards and two Managing Governors appointed by the Government of India on the recommendation of the Central Board, holding office for such periods as the Government of India directs from time to time.

Until the establishment of the Reserve Bank of India in 1935 the Imperial Bank was discharging the main central banking functions as:

1. Acting as Sole Banker to government and as custodian of public funds and government cash balances, control local and also of the balance of secretary of State through its London office.
2. Undertaking the function arising from the issue of new loans by the government and managing the public debt in return for a specified remuneration.
3. Giving public facilities for the transfer of money between in branches; at rates approved by the Controller of Currency.
4. In addition to these central banking functions, the Bank performed the ordinary commercial banking business of accepting deposits, making loans and advances, remitting money from one place to another and keeping safe deposits etc. Certain restrictions were imposed by government on its ordinary commercial banking functions like the bank was prohibited from making loans for a longer period than six months or on the basis of immovable property or on the security of its own shares or stocks, from discounting or making loans against any bill unless it carries the several responsibilities of at least two persons or firms unconnected with each other in financial partnership. The Bank was statutorily debarred from dealing in foreign exchange business except to meet the bonafide needs of its own clients.

With the establishment of the Reserve Bank of India in 1935, the Imperial Bank ceased to be the banker to the government directly. Further the Imperial Bank of India Amendment Act 1934, removed all the restrictions which were formerly imposed on its lending operations. Under the Amendment Act the Bank could transact foreign exchange business and undertake banking business of any kind. It could make loans and advances for periods exceeding six months on the basis of immovable property as also on its own share. With the establishment of the Reserve Bank of India, although the Imperial Bank of India ceased to be the Banker to the Government directly, it was authorised to act as the sole agent of the Reserve Bank of India in places where the latter did not have its branches. Accordingly, the Imperial Bank was permitted on behalf of government to pay, receive, collect and remit money, bullion and securities as the agent for Reserve Bank of India and to undertake and transact another business which Reserve Bank of India may from time to time, entrust to the Bank. Thus, the Imperial Bank of India stood on a special category and it was the Bank of the Indian Money Market.

When the question of the nationalisation of the Imperial Bank of India came up first in February 1948, the Government accepted the principle of Nationalisation. But this was opposed by Central Board of Directors and shareholders. They put forward many arguments against Nationalisation and ultimately the Government announced in 1949 the indefinite postponement of the question of Nationalisation of the Imperial Bank of India. But the question came up again when the All India Rural Credit Committee recommended the creation of the State Bank of India by amalgamation of certain state owned Banks with the Imperial Bank. The day July 1, 1955 was the landmark day when SBI came into existence. Thus, the State Bank of India was established by statutory amalgamation of the Imperial Bank of India and certain major associated banks viz. Bank of Saurashtra, Bank of Patiala, Bank of Bikaner, Bank of Jaipur, Bank of Indore, Bank of Baroda, Bank of Mysore, The Hyderabad Bank and Travancore Bank. The branches of these Banks alongwith the branches of the Imperial Bank of India would have a larger coverage of several areas and also a greater scope for making larger future extension to rural areas. That is why the Rural Banking Enquiry Committee stated in its report that "If these banks could be integrated into the institution, and that one institution could be aligned to the national problems, then that would be an extremely important and extremely desirable line of development." Thus, the nationalisation of the Imperial Bank and establishment of the State Bank of India was an important milestone on the road to the establishment of an integrated commercial banking unit with branches all over the country under an effective State Control.

The establishment of the SBI was visualised as fundamental reform by the All India Rural Credit Survey Committee that was not only fundamental and indeed inevitable in relation to important aspects of the national policy but also capable of serving a number of other important national purposes. It was in fact the beginning of the process of reshaping the commercial banking system of the country so as to make it an instrument of the national policy which culminated in the nationalisation of 14 major banks in July 1969. The specific purposes for which the establishment of the bank was recommended were to spread banking facilities in rural areas through an expanded network of offices, to conduct cash work of the government and the provide remittance facilities to cooperative and other banks. Achievements of these objectives by themselves would not have met the criterion of a fundamental reform. The substance of the findings of the All India Rural Credit Survey was that commercial banks had bypassed the major sections of the Indian economy viz. agriculture, small scale industry and small business. Planned economic development of the country however required these sectors contributing, as they did, the bulk of national income. It was expected that SBI would do the pioneering work in this respect.

The SBI inherited from its predecessor, the Imperial Bank of India, a branch network, policy orientation, systems and procedures which were attuned to financing of large scale industry and trade. There was much strength in this heritage. The tremendous expansion in organisation and operation recorded over the last three decades by the SBI was possible mainly because the system and procedures as also the quality of the staff were of a high order and could stand the strain of the rapid expansion, however, change was most necessary and was brought about in a systematic manner. In the initial period, changes required in staff orientation and in the schemes of financing were necessarily imposed from the top; these were the responses of the top management to the requirement of the national policy. In a few years, the trial and error of the earlier years had resulted in the implementation of a mechanism of charge and adaption in the organisation structure of the bank. It is a well known fact that the first major step towards introducing commercial banks in agriculture lending was the creation of the State Bank of India in July 1955. Assigned a major responsibility of extending banking facilities in rural and urban areas, the SBI and its associates between 1955 and 1969 had opened 1737 offices of which 784 (40.5%) were in rural areas with a population of less than 10,000. This creditable performance, in a way, could be taken as indirectly responsible for the tasks entrusted to the commercial bank after nationalisation from the angle of extending assistance to the co-operative by way of providing cheap remittance facilities and financing marketing and processing co-operative societies as also subscribing to the debentures of land mortgage banks, the contribution of the SBI was considerable. Again as early as in 1964, the State Bank of India had through its Rural Pilot centres schemes envisaged financing of cultivators directly in the select rural areas. Thus, in more than one ways, the SBI as the premier banking institution in the country in the field of Agriculture, the pace of rural banking in terms of branch expansion as well as quality and quantity of lending was thus set by SBI. By 1969 when most others were entering the fields, the SBI had not only made significant headway but had also commenced refining its approval and seeking innovations. Moreover, the experience of financing individual farmers in scattered areas led to the realisation that what was needed by them was a package of credit as also supporting extension services. Thus, the bank looked for an approach which would ensure an effective as well as intensive coverage of a large number of farmers. This was the genesis of the Bank's Area approach an approach which involves selection of a compact as well as contiguous area comprising a cluster of villages and extending need based credit to all viable and potentially viable farmers in that area. Such an approach also facilitated the formulation of integrated area development schemes benefits of which could be reaped by a larger number of people. But that could be termed as a major cause for formulating such an approach, the desire to provide the small/marginal farmers and other weaker sections of the society with a variety of services apart from mere provision of credit. To these small farmers who have to play a crucial role in increasing agriculture production through adoption of intensive cultivation methods under the new strategy, provision of vital inputs at the appropriate time and in adequate quantities, technical assistance and guidance were considered by the SBI to be as necessary as providing financial assistance. Having adopted this approach, the SBI went ahead in its search for instruments to translate this approach and its benefits into action. The results came in the shape of two further innovations.

The agricultural development branches and the village adoption scheme-creation of these Agriculture Development branches is a new experiment without a parallel in the history of rural banking in India. Equipped with the required complement to technical and non-technical staff these branches commenced with definite business plans for 4-5 years designed to achieve a credit dispersal target of Rs 1 crore to Rs 1.50 crores over an area of 100 to 125 villages. The other innovation viz. the Village Adoption Scheme Approach essentially an extension of the idea of the area approach. The branches select a village or a cluster of villages after conducting a detailed survey of the potential and in consultation with the department/ agencies, villages so selected come under intensive financing aimed at not only covering nil viable and potential viable farmers but also through special area development schemes.

The bank had to make arrangement in short time for the recruitment of trained technical personnel to handle the growing requirement of agriculture financing. As a further extension of the area approach/village adoption programme, the concept of integrated rural development programme fulfilling not only the economic needs but also catering the social and cultural needs of the villages is a recent step in the banks strategies. Envisaged with the idea of active cooperation with various other agencies - government, semi-government, voluntary organisations as well as business houses - these programmes encompass plans catering to almost the total requirements of the rural population. The role of the SBI has thus been enlarged from a mere credit purveying agency to that of a sponsoring agency committee to the task of all round rural development in selected areas. This speaks of the strides that SBI has made in its service to the nation. Simultaneously alternative methods of financing are also being actively pursued by the bank. Conscious of the limitations in the organisational set up, financing through intermediaries like primary agriculture credit societies and farmers service societies, etc. also receive as much attention. Right from the beginning, the SBI has been a major and active partner in the implementation of this scheme. Four decades of the post-independence planning have not only served to stress this fact but also reinforce it to a promise which is almost irrefutable.

The first effort in provision of credit for agriculture through institution sources could be traced to the cooperative movement in the country at the beginning of this century. Though their performance picked up of the years that followed, the growing demand for credit particularly after the adoption of the intensive cultivation strategy in the early sixties, underlined the need for the participation of other Institutional agencies in this task. Commercial banks were considered to be one of the major sources to meet the demand for credit. Until two decades ago, commercial banks lended to shy away from financing agriculture operation and were mainly concerned with financing trading and industrial ventures. The rising demand for credit, the urgency of the problem as well as changes in the government policy led to their increasing involvement in the national task-the growth of agriculture production.

Three major measures were catalytic in ensuring their active participation. These were - (1) the constitution of the SBI in July by nationalising the Imperial Bank of India, (2) the schemes of social centre in 1968 and (3) the nationalisation of 14 major commercial banks in 1969.

The object behind these measures was to provide banking facilities in rural areas and so far neglected sectors like agriculture and small scale industries.

New Banking Policy

The nationalised banks are expected to perform much more than merely mobilising the community's savings for purpose of lending to a few selected sectors. Under New Banking Policy loans are purpose worthy instead of security worthy. The purpose of the loan sanctioned is to be of prime importance. Under the old policy adequate security would have justified a loan even for a project of doubtful viability.

Traditionally, a banker hardly bothered about the financial analysis and need of the borrower once he is certain about the safety and security offered for the loan. But now a banker advances only when he is satisfied about the genuineness of the financial need of the party. The assessment of genuineness is only possible after analyzing the party's past and projected balance sheet and financial records on objective basis. Hence subjectivity base is changed into objectivity base in the event of advances to borrowers.

After nationalisation, the banks have to act as agents of growth in various areas. Under lead bank scheme various banks are surveying the socio-economic resources of the areas allotted to them i.e. not only they collect deposits and advance it to the borrowers but also identify the potentiality of the area.

On the eve of nationalisation there were regional disparities in the share of various states both in total bank deposits and advances. The post nationalisation banking policies is concerned with removal of disparities in deposit and advances. The new banking policy aims at correcting the past sectoral imbalances of bank credit by diverting on increasingly large share of new advances towards the priority sectors i.e. agriculture, small scale industries, retail trade, exports, small business, self employed people, education etc.

The innovative banking activities were initiated by nationalised bank in response to social needs, especially to meet the growing aspirations of common man. The bank can ensure the implications of change in banking trend only by introducing the system of business planning or affecting the system. Head office determines their multi-dimensional goals and translates these goals in budget figures of advances and deposits or by opening of new branches in each region. Similarly regional manager assesses the business potentialities in the area, then bank's branches provide foundation budget. In this way whole budgeting process is pushed up from branches to Regional offices and ultimately to the head office.

So under the new banking policy:

(i) The purpose of the loan sanctioned is of prime importance.

(ii) It should always be for productive and not for speculative purposes even if adequate security is available for the latter.

(iii) Banks should normally lend for such proposals which are technically feasible, financially sound and economically viable. Under the old policy, adequate security would have justified a loan even for a project of doubtful viability but now such a project cannot qualify for a bank loan.

(iv) Traditionally a banker would have hardly bothered about the financial analysis and need of the borrower once he was certain about the safety and security offered for the loan in question. But under the new banking policy a banker should not advance a loan merely on the basis of security offered unless he is satisfied about the genuineness of the financial need of the party. The assessment on genuine need is to be done on an objective basis after analyzing the party's past and projected balance sheets and financial records. Hence the element of subjectivity and arbitrariness has now given way to an objective and scientific analysis of the borrower's record before lending to him.

(v) In the past a bank loan was normally available for working capital. The assumption was that party would manage the funds for investment in fixed assets from its own sources or from the market. Such an attitude precluded the possibility of setting up of a modern business by a man of meager means even if he was highly talented and professionally competent. Only such persons who were capable of investing in fixed assets from their own resources or those whose credit in the market was high enough to float shares or debentures in the market successfully and deploy it for acquiring fixed assets, were only eligible to approach commercial banks for working capital finance.

(vi) Moreover need is branch banking instead of unit banking. Branches in India had only a limited role to play in the past. The majority of the branches were opened in the past in prosperous areas so that they could succeed in collecting maximum deposits from that area and transmit the funds so collected to their respective Head Office/Central Office if 'traditional clientels' did not pre-exist in the common area of that branch. This trick worked well till sixties.

But during late sixties the realisation grew all over the country that a commercial bank is certainly not a deposit collector like a post office or the government department. It is something more than that and no branch can afford to ignore the genuine aspirations of the people of its command area.

(vii) After nationalisation it was specifically spelled out by the government that the nationalised banks would have to act as agents of growth in various areas where their branches already exist or would be opened in future. In fact, under the lead bank scheme various banks were entrusted with the job of surveying the socio-economic resources of the districts allocated to them so that they could take appropriate action for the development of these districts. Thus under the current banking policy, lead banks are not only to collect deposits and advance to prospective borrower, but have to survey the area, identify the potentiality of the area, formulate appropriate project for the area, select the correct persons for executing those projects, finance the project singly or in consortium with other banks of the district through the leverage of district consultative committees.

Thus, the nationalised banks are expected to perform much more than merely mobilising the community's savings for the purpose of lending to a few selected sectors. The Head office/central office of each bank can ensure proper execution of the aforesaid new policies only by introducing the system of business planning i.e. system.

Top executives at central office determine their multidimensional goals. They are to figure out these goals in budget figures of advances and deposits or opening of new branches in each region in consultation with regional managers on the basis of factoral information supplied by them.

Similarly the regional manager assess the business potentialities of their region on the basis of data and information supplied by their respective branches and supplement it by their personal impressions about additional business potentialities in the area by opening new branches. Evidently in this process the formulation budgets are provided by the bank branch and the whole banking process is pushed up from branch to regional office and ultimately to the head office.

The understanding of organisational structure of SBI is a precondition for appreciating the mechanics of the system at Central office. Head Office/ Regional Office level branches are at the grass root of the organisational structure. This is the ultimate analysis. It is the branches who prepare their own respective budget based on their staff and environmental potentialities to enable the branches to prepare acceptable budgets. The Local Head office's concern is to convey them the organisation's goal and their expectations.

HO/RO get their ideas (in terms about the goals and expectations of Central Office, which in turn is based on government's policy and environmental analysis of entire country.

Formulation of Central Office Policy Guidelines

In the system all the branches send their budget to the Regional Office and likeness budgets of Regions are transmitted to Head Office. It is a grass root system because branch at grass roots know the business potentialities of their respective areas. But branches or Regional office cannot make the system unless they have some understanding of the Head Office level or we can say directions of Head Office or top management is necessary for proper preparation of budgeting at grass root level. The branches and Regional Office need some guidelines from their head office for preparing performance budgets.

Preparation of guidelines of SBI Head Office is as under:

(1) Senior Executives at the head office (including economic aid and other experts relating to Agriculture, Small Scale Industries, Large Industries, Trade etc.) are requested to prepare working papers related to expected additions in

deposits and advances to various sectors in each region during coming year. This exercise is done keeping in view the past trend of business in each segment as well as the likely economic, regulatory and other current factors at the macro level which may affect the bank business in the coming year.

(2) The working papers thus prepared are then consolidated and crystallised into draft policy guidelines for sectoral performances in various regions. In the final analysis, guidelines are formulated for the guidance of the various regions.

(3) The draft guidelines are then discussed with the members of the top management team i.e. the Managing Director, Central Manager, Deputy General Manager etc. So that expectation of top management regarding the desired level of sectoral achievement in various circles may be fulfilled.

(4) Simultaneously each region is requested to collect similar data related to their business and general environment for their own region. The idea is to identify the business potentialities at various regions/ branches.

(5) Now the Regional Managers are invited by Head Office for a meeting with Managing Director and other senior executives with a view to finalise the Central Office's policy guidelines for each region. Evidently the Regional Managers are fully involved at the stage of formulation and finalisation of Central policy guidelines.

(6) The final Head Office policy guidelines are then sent to each region. The latter in turn may formulate its own guidelines. The regional policy guidelines must obviously be consistent with Central policy guidelines.

(7) The Regional policy guidelines are then sent to various branches alongwith printed performance budget sheet with a request to prepare budget in conformity with these guidelines.

Such process of budgeting is based on Head Office's guidelines on one hand and the business potentiality of the branches and regions on the other.

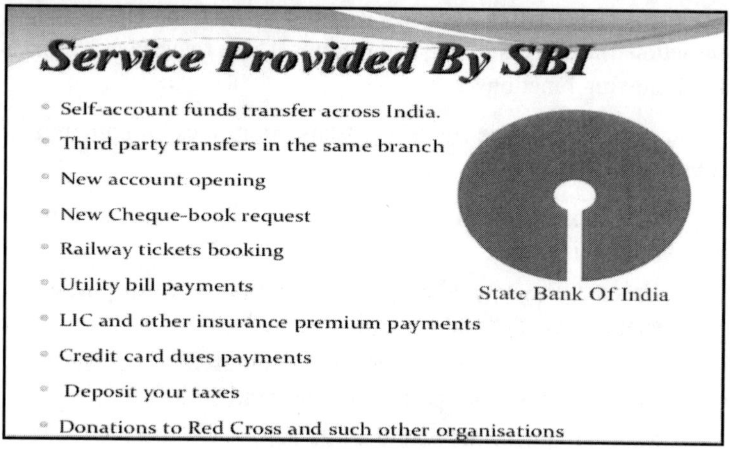

Figure 12 : SBI E-Banking Services.

SBI E-Banking Services

Retail Banking:

The Retail banking application is an integration of several functional areas, and enables customers to:

- Issue Demand Drafts online.
- Transfer funds to own and third party accounts.
- Credit beneficiary accounts using the VISA Money Transfer, RTGS/ NEFT feature.
- Generate account statements.
- Setup Standing Instructions.
- Configure profile settings.
- Use e-Tax for online tax payment.
- Use e-Pay for automatic bill payments.
- Interface with merchants for railway and airline reservations
- Avail DEMAT and IPO services.

Corporate Banking

The Online SBI corporate banking application provides features to administer and manage corporate accounts online. The corporate module provides roles such as Regulator, Admin, Uploader, Transaction Maker, Authoriser, and Auditor. These roles have access to the following functions:

Manage users, define rights and transaction rules on corporate accounts:

- Access accounts in several branches with a single sign-on mechanism.
- Upload files to make bulk transactions to third parties, supplier, vendor and tax collection authorities.
- Use online transactional features such as fund transfer to own accounts, third party payments, and draft issues.
- Make bill payments over the Internet.
- Authorise, modify, reschedule and cancel transactions, based on rights assigned to the user.
- Generate account statement.
- Enquire on transaction details or current balance.

Value Added Services

- Tax payments to central and state governments through site to site integration.
- Supply Chain Finance (e-VFS- Electronic Vendor Finance Scheme).
- Direct Debit Facility.
- E Collection Facilities for:
- Core Banking Transactions.
- Internet Bank transactions for incoming RTGS/NEFT Transactions.
- Internet banking transactions for SBI and associate banks.
- Debit facility where suppliers can directly debit their customer's account through internet banking.

Products and Services

- E-Ticketing

- SBI E-Tax
- Bill Payment
- RTGS/NEFT
- E-Payment
- Fund Transfer
- Third Party Transfer
- Demand Draft
- Cheque Book Request
- Account Opening Request
- Account Statement
- Transaction Enquiry
- Demat Account Statement
- Donation

E-Ticketing

You can book your railway, air and bus tickets online through Online SBI.

To book your train ticket, just log on to irctc.co.in and create an ID there at if you do not have one. Submit your travel plan and book the ticket(s) - either i-ticket (where the delivery of tickets will be made at your address) or E-tickets (wherein after successful payment transactions, an e-ticket is generated which can be printed any time. For an e-ticket, the details of photo identity card will required to be filled in) and select State Bank of India in the payment options. You will be redirected to Internet Banking site of SBI (www.onlinesbi.com). After submitting the respective ID and password, you can select your account. After a successful debit, Railways will generate the ticket. E-ticket can be printed by you whereas the i-ticket will be dispatched by IRCTC at the given address. Service charges @ Rs 10/ - per transaction shall be levied in addition to the cost of the ticket. Cancellation of E-ticket can be done by logging on to IRCTC's site; refund amount will be credited to your account directly within 2 - 3 days. For cancellation of i-ticket, you shall be required to submit your ticket at a computerised counter of

Railways and on cancellation; the amount shall be credited back to your account.

You can also book your Air ticket through the e-ticketing feature.

Log on to Indian Airlines website to make a payment for an e-ticket through State Bank of India, you need to select SBI as the payment option. The payment request will be redirected to Internet Banking site. The request may be processed based on values sent from the airlines website.

Once a transaction is processed, an appropriate response will be sent to airlines site to update the status of the transaction. You can print the E-ticket immediately.

To book bus tickets to destinations in Karnataka, log on to the KSRTC website. Provide details about the start and end points of your journey, date of journey and number of tickets. Verify availability of seats on the selected date and confirm the transaction. Select "Online SBI" to make the payment. Provide your credentials and select the SBI account that will be debited for the payment. You are provided a KSRTC reference number for your e-Ticket.

SBI E-Tax

You can pay your taxes online through SBI E-Tax. This facility enables you to pay TDS, Income tax, Indirect tax, Corporation tax, Wealth tax, Estate Duty and Fringe Benefits tax.

Click the e-Tax link in the home page. You are displayed a page with two links Direct Tax and Indirect Tax.

Click the Direct Tax link. You will be redirected to the NSDL site where you can select an online challan based on the tax you wish to pay. Provide the PAN, name and address, assessment year, nature of payment and bank name. On selecting the bank name as SBI and submitting the form, you will be redirected to the Internet Banking site. After submitting the respective ID and password, you can select your account for making payment of taxes. After payment is successful you can print the E-Receipt for the payment.

The E-receipt can be printed at a later date also and the same can be retrieved from:

Enquiries > Find Transactions > Status Enquiries > Click on the respective transaction to print the tax receipt.

Bill Payment

- A simple and convenient service for viewing and paying your bills online.
- No more late payments.
- No more queues.
- No more hassles of depositing cheques.

Using the bill payment you can view and pay various bills online, directly from your SBI account. You can pay telephone, electricity, insurance, credit cards and other bills from the comfort of your house or office, 24 hours a day, 365 days a year. Simply logon to http://www.onlinesbi.com/ with your credentials and register the biller to which you want to pay, with all the bill details. Once the bill is uploaded by the biller, you can make payment online.

RTGS/NEFT

You can transfer money from your State Bank account to accounts in other banks using the RTGS/NEFT service. The RTGS system facilitates transfer of funds from accounts in one bank to another on a "real time" and on "gross settlement" basis. This system is the fastest possible interbank money transfer facility available through secure banking channels in India. RTGS transaction requests will be sent to RBI immediately during working hours post working hours requests are registered and sent to RBI on next working day. You can also schedule a transaction for a future date. You can transfer an amount of Rs 1 lac and above using RTGS system.

NEFT

National Electronic Funds Transfer (NEFT) facilitates transfer of funds to the credit account with the other participating bank.

RBI acts as the service provider and transfers the credit to the other bank's account.

E-Payment

You can pay your insurance premium, mobile phone bills and also you can purchase mutual fund units by coming from the biller's website and selecting State Bank of India in the payment option.

LIC Premium

For paying premium of LIC policy log on to www.licindia.com and register your policy details. When the premium is due select State Bank of India in the make payment option.

SBI Mutual Fund

You can invest in the SBI Mutual Fund schemes online. Log on to www.sbimf.com and select the scheme in which you want to make investment in the payment option select State Bank of India.

CC Avenue

Enjoy shopping at the CC Avenue Shopping Mall and purchase from a wide variety of products and services through CC Avenue Certified Vendors. Make payments for your purchases using your Internet enabled SBI accounts.

Fund Transfer

The Funds Transfer facility enables you to transfer funds within your accounts in the same branch or other branches. You can transfer aggregating Rs 1 lakh per day to own accounts in the same branch and other branches. To make a funds transfer, you should be an active Internet Banking user with transaction rights. Funds transfer to PPF account is restricted to the same branch. Just log on to retail section of the Internet Banking site with your credentials and select the Funds Transfer link under Payments/Transfers tab. You can see all your online debit and credit accounts. Select the debit account from which you wish to transfer funds and the credit account into which the amount is to be credited. Enter the amount and remarks. The remarks will be displayed in your accounts statement for this transaction. You will be displayed the last five funds transfer operations on your accounts. On confirming the transaction, you will be displayed a confirmation page with the details of the transaction and the option to submit or cancel the funds transfer request. A reference number will be generated for your record.

How to Activate Internet Banking

Internet Banking adds up many ways ease the facility of banking. Receiving or paying money in secure and easy way is the key features of internet banking. Just recall olden days, when people had to queue up at banking counters for withdrawing money, or for paying even pity expenses. Fear about mischievous act was the genuine issue at that time. But the advent of internet and after than net banking removes the miserable condition of common man. Now common men are much more relieved in terms of transaction security and convenience. Paying government sponsored taxes as well as utility bills are not longer tough exercise today.

In India State Bank of India has already introduced internet banking. Any one having bank account in SBI may use thc facility of net banking. In order to activate SBI Net Banking account holders have to take following steps to get permission for it.

SBI Internet Banking Activation Process

- Download application form from thc official website of State Bank of India **(Online SBI).** Fill it up and submit to the branch where you have an account and internet banking is running there. Online application form for internet banking activation can be downloaded by visiting SBI Internet Banking Registration Form.
- You may visit SBI branch office first and ask for internet banking form.
- After 1-2 week from the date of submission of application the password in a secure envelope will be reached to you. This envelope is send by courier to your given address.

ONLINE SBI
REGISTRATION FORM

To
The Branch Manager
State Bank of India
....

I wish to register as a user of 'OnlineSBI', SBI's Internet Banking Service.

Name of Customer **(25 Characters)**

Mobile Number: +91

E-Mail:

Date of Birth: DD MM YY

My Account Numbers	Single/ Joint* Accounts	(Branch Use) Transaction Rights (Y/N)	(Branch Use) ** Limited Transaction Rights (Y/N)

* **Rights on the OnLineSBI Service will be same as that in your account at the branch.**
** **Transaction rights to transfer funds within own CIF, e-TDR/e-STDR and new a/c opening request through branch intervention**

I have read the provisions contained in the "Terms of Service (Terms & Conditions) document" of "OnlineSBI" and accept them. I agree that the transactions executed over OnlineSBI under my Username and Password will be binding on me.

Customer's Signature Date:

For SBI Internet Banking First Time User:-

Before making first time login for SBI Internet Banking remember to use internet explorer browser to login and change the password.

- First time user for new registration login to **SBI Internet Banking First Time Login.**
- Now you are needed to login SBI online banking website for this you have to visit the website at given web address: **SBI Internet Banking Login.**
- Here click the login button.
- From here you will go to a new page. Here click on continue to login.
- Now login page is in front of you. Here you have to login with the received password and change it to your on user name and password. This is mandatory. So, I will suggest that right on your password and user name on plain paper, then start logging in. Fill up received user name and password and click login.

Rules and Regulations of Internet Banking:

General Information:

1. The Online SBI Global registration form(s) should be addressed and sent directly to the branch where the applicant(s) maintain his/her/ their account(s).
2. Separate registration is required in case the accounts are maintained at different branches. Separate registration is allowed for single and joint accounts at your option.
3. Normally you can access your accounts through the Online SBI Global only after you acknowledge to the respective branch(es) the receipt of the User Name and Password sent to you.
4. Each account holder in a joint account with "Either or Survivor" type mode of operation may register himself / herself as a user of the Online SBI Global facility.

5. All other accounts not listed in the registration form will be available on the OnlineSBIGlobal for the purpose of enquiry only. The customers may approach Branch for enabling transaction rights on such accounts any time.
6. The OnlineSBIGlobal service cannot be claimed as a right. The Bank may also convert the Service into a discretionary service (being a service which may be discontinued by the Bank) anytime, if so warranted, after it has been made available to you. The Bank may also impose and vary any restrictions on the use of OnlineSBIGlobal at any time including any minimum and maximum daily limits for transactions effected over it.
7. Transactions over the internet may be subject to interruption, transmission blackout, delayed transmission due to internet traffic, or incorrect data transmission due to the public nature of the internet. The Bank cannot assume responsibility for malfunctions in communications facilities not under our control that may affect the accuracy or timeliness of messages you send.
8. The OnlineSBIGlobal is offered only in jurisdictions where and when it may be lawfully offered. OnlineSBIGlobal and information relating to OnlineSBIGlobal are not intended for access or use by persons in other jurisdictions.

Hardware Based Security Tokens – One Time Password Generators:

1. The security token is personal to you and can only be used with your password. It provides an additional level of security for certain transactions and cannot be shared with anyone else.
2. Once activated, you will need to commence using the one time security token when you use Online SBI Global. You will need to enter the code displayed (once per session) on the security token when you: • add a third party beneficiary • send funds to a third party beneficiary.

3. You can choose to cancel your security token at any time by contacting the Bank.
4. You must keep your security token safe and secure and advise the Bank immediately if it is lost, stolen or misused. Until the Bank's actual receipt of such notification, the Customer shall remain responsible for any and all use of the Online SBI Global by un-authorised persons or for un-authorised purposes. The Bank will deactivate your security token and arrange for a replacement one to be sent to you. A security token replacement fee will apply. Refer to our 'Schedule of Fees and Charges' on www.sbihongkong.com for details.
5. If you have any questions about the security token, please call the Bank between 9.00 am and 5.00 pm, Monday to Friday.
6. The Bank makes no representation or warranty on the quality, merchantability or fitness for purpose of the security token and accepts no liability for any loss or damage incurred or suffered by you arising from your failure to safe keep or use the security token in accordance with the Bank's instructions.

Bank's Terms

1. All requests received from you shall be logged and transmitted to your branch for their fulfillment. The requests become effective from the time these are recorded / registered at the respective branch. While registering the request, you shall be informed about the time normally taken by the Bank for fulfillment of such requests.
2. The rules and regulations applicable to the banking transactions done in traditional way at the Hong Kong branch of State Bank of India will be applicable for the transactions done through the Online SBI Global service.
3. Disputes between the registered user of this service and the Bank with regard to the transactions done through Online SBI Global will be subject to the jurisdiction of the Court of Hong Kong (where the branch maintaining the relative account of the user is located) and will be governed by Hong Kong law in force from time to time.

4. The Bank will take reasonable care to make use of the available technology for ensuring security and preventing unauthorised access to any of the services offered through the Online SBI Global.
5. The Online SBI Global service is a VeriSign-certified secure site. VeriSign assures that during the session you are dealing with website of SBI, the two-way communication is secured with 128-bit SSL encryption technology, which ensures the confidentiality of the data during transmission. The access-control methods designed on the site afford a high level of security to the transactions conducted on Online SBI Global.
6. The Bank reserves the right to modify, change, add or cancel any of the services offered through Online SBI Global without prior notice to the Users or the Terms of Service listed in this Document by reasonable prior notice to you. The changes will be notified to you / customers through a notification on the site.
7. The Bank does not warrant or represent that the Online SBI Global is free from virus or other destructive features which may adversely affect your hardware, software or equipment.

Your Obligations:

1. Password of your choice must replace the Password given by the Bank at the time of FIRST log-in. This is Mandatory.
2. You are free to choose the Password of your choice as per the guidelines on the site. However, you are advised to avoid choosing a password that is generic in nature, guessable / inferable from the personal data such as name, date of birth, address, telephone number, driving license / car number etc. You should not use the Password for accessing other services (for example, connection to the internet or accessing other websites).
3. You are welcome to access Online SBI Global from anywhere anytime where it is legal to do so in the relevant place. However, as a matter of precaution and safety, you should avoid using PCs with public access.

4. There is no way to retrieve the Password from the system. In case you forget your Password, you will have to approach the branch to reset the password.
5. You must keep the User Name and Password strictly confidential and known only to himself / herself. You should destroy the original printed copy of the User Name and Password, should not allow anyone else to use the User Name and Password, should not write down the User Name or Password on any device for accessing the Online SBI Global service or on anything usually kept with or near it, and should not write down or record the User Name or Password without disguising it. You should refer to the security advice provided by the Bank from time to time. The Bank will not be responsible for any loss sustained by you arising out of a breach of this condition.
6. The Bank presupposes that log-in using valid User Name and Password is a valid session initiated by none other than you to whom the said Username and Password belong.
7. All transactions executed through a valid session as defined above will be construed to have been emanated from you and will be legally binding on you. You are cautioned against leaving the computer unattended during a valid session.
8. Should you notice that any information relating to your account(s) is incorrect or discrepant the same should be immediately brought to the notice of the branch (es) by telephone.
9. You must inform the Bank as soon as reasonably practicable by telephone if you find or believe that your Username or Password has been compromised, lost or stolen, or that unauthorised transactions have been conducted over the account.
10. You will not attempt or permit others to attempt accessing Online SBI Global through any unlawful means or use or attempt to use Online SBI Global for any unlawful purposes.

11. You shall not, and shall not attempt to decompile, reverse-engineer, translate, convert, adapt, alter, modify, enhance, add to, delete or in any way tamper with, or gain access to, any part of Online SBI Global or any internet site or any software comprised in it.

Your Liabilities

1. You shall not be responsible for any direct loss suffered by you as a result of unauthorised transactions conducted through Online SBI Global service unless you act fraudulently or with gross negligence such as failure to properly safeguard your Username, Password or security token.
2. You shall be liable for all losses if you have acted fraudulently or with gross negligence. You will be considered as having acted with gross negligence if you knowingly allows the use by others of your Username, Password or security token or fail to follow the safeguards set out in this Document.
3. In the absence of negligence, fraud or fault on your part, you shall not be liable for loss or misplacement of funds caused by unauthorised transactions effected through use of Online SBI Global as a result of (a) a computer crime not prevented by the Bank's security; (b) a human or system error caused by the Bank, resulting in an improper transaction, leading to lost or misplaced funds, or (c) a missed or mis-directed payment caused by the Bank.

REFERENCES

1. Allison, Theodore Edward. "A Comparative Study of Bank Performance under Branch and Unit System", Ph. D Thesis (University of Illinois at Urbana, 2001).
2. Satish Munjal. "Performance Budgeting as Control Tool in the Hands of Management," Maharashtra Co-operative Journal, Pune (Jan-March 1984).
3. Satish Munjal. "Performance Budgeting & Monitoring Progress in Banks in India", Indian Management, (November, 1984).
4. Satish Munjal. "Performance Budgeting and Manpower Planning", Maharashtra Co-operative Journal, Pune (April 1985).
5. Muranjan, S.K. "Modern Banking in India" (Bombay, Himalaya Pub. House).

6. Basu, S.K. "Recent Banking development", Delhi, S. Chand, 2002.
7. Basu, A.K. "Fundamentals of Banking Theory and Practice" Delhi, S. Chand, 2002.
8. Birla Institute of Scientific Mgt. "Banks since Nationalisation" (Allied Pub. Pvt. Ltd., 2002).
9. Economic Survey (Delhi, Government of India), Various issues.
10. Report of Trend and Progress of Banking in India (Bombay, Reserve Bank of India), Various Issues.
11. SBI, Monthly Reports, P & D Department, Central Office, SBI, Bombay.
12. SBI—Plan and its fulfillment, July 1955/June 1960, Annual Reports on trends and progress of Banking in India, Central Office, Bombay.
13. Reports of All India Rural Credit Committee.
14. Economic Survey (Delhi, Government of India), Various issues.

Chapter - VI

Profile and E-banking Services of HDFC

HDFC Profile

The Housing Development Finance Corporation Limited (HDFC) was amongst the first to receive an 'in principle' approval from the Reserve Bank of India (RBI) to set up a bank in the private sector, as part of the RBI's liberalisation of the Indian Banking Industry in 1994. The bank was incorporated in August 1994 in the name of 'HDFC Bank Limited', with its registered office in Mumbai, India. HDFC Bank commenced its operations as a Scheduled Commercial Bank in January 1995.

HDFC Bank comprises of a dynamic and enthusiastic team determined to accomplish the vision of becoming a World-class Indian bank. HDFC bank's business philosophy is based on our four core values - Customer Focus, Operational Excellence, Product Leadership and People. They believe that the ultimate identity and success of their bank will reside in the exceptional quality of people and their extraordinary efforts. They are committed to hiring, developing, motivating and retaining the best people in the industry.

HDFC was incorporated in the year 1977, but it started its activities in Jaipur only from 21st March, 2002 with its prime objective of promoting home ownership by providing long term finance to households for their housing needs in Rajasthan and particularly in Jaipur.

When HDFC started their business activities in Jaipur, there was no other organisation which was catering to the needs of the people for housing purposes in specific, except some commercial banks. Franchise's money lenders and LIC.

They entered in the market when Jaipur had started moving towards rapid growth and development, due to which economic, business financial and social activities changed.

There was growth in business activities with the industrialisation of the country and subsequently the state, shifting of families from the scenario of joint family system to unitary family led to increase in demand for housing finance the same effect was caused by the room in tourism industry not only in Jaipur but also in Rajasthan as a whole and these needs and demands of the people were met by operation of HDFC.

Housing finance in Jaipur has undergone a second revolution where the specialised lenders continue to play an important role. Commercial banks are gradually emerging as mortgage lenders and many more are entering in these rapidly changing times companies had to be more aware of their true comparative and competitive advantages, develop their strengths in a more focused manner to succeed in a more competitive environment. Predicting and anticipating future trends with preparedness would make the company profitable.

Progress of HDFC Bank

On May 23, 2008, the amalgamation of Centurion Bank of Punjab with HDFC Bank was formally approved by Reserve Bank of India to complete the statutory and regulatory approval process. As per the scheme of amalgamation, shareholder of CBOP received 1 share of HDFC Bank for every 29 shares of CBOP. The merged entity will have a strong deposit base of around Rs 1,22,000 crore and net advances of around Rs 89,000 crore. The balance sheet size of the combined entity would be over Rs 1,63,000 crore. The amalgamation added significant value to HDFC Bank in terms of increased branch network, geographic reach, and customer base, and a bigger pool of skilled manpower. In a milestone transaction in the Indian banking industry. Times Bank Limited (another new private sector bank promoted by Bennett, Coleman & Co. / Times Group) was merged with HDFC Bank Ltd., effective February 26, 2000.This was the first merger of two private banks in the New Generation Private Sector

Banks. As per the scheme of amalgamation approved by the shareholders of both banks and the Reserve Bank of India, shareholders of Times Bank received 1 share of HDFC Bank for every 5.75 shares of Times Bank.

HDFC Bank is headquartered in Mumbai. The Bank at present has an enviable network of 1,725 branches spread in 780 cities across India. All branches are linked on an online real time basis. Customers in over 500 locations are also serviced through Telephone Banking. The Bank's expansion plans take into account the need to have a presence in all major industrial and commercial centres where its corporate customers are located as well as the need to build a strong retail customer base for both deposits and loan products. Being a clearing / settlement bank to various leading stock exchanges, the Bank has branches in the centres where the NSE /BSE have a strong and active member base. The Bank also has 5,231 networked ATMs across these cities. Moreover, HDFC Bank's ATM network can be accessed by all domestic and international Visa / Master Card, Visa Electron/ Maestro, Plus / Circus and American Express Credit / Charge Cardholders.

HDFC has always been market-oriented and dynamic with respect to resource mobilisation as well as its lending programme. This renders it more than capable to meet the new challenges that have emerged. Over the years, HDFC has developed a vast client base of borrowers, depositors, shareholders and agents, and it hopes to capitalise on this loyal and satisfied client base for future growth. Internal systems have been developed to be robust and agile, to take into account changes in the volatile external environment.

HDFC has developed a network of institutions through partnerships with some of the best institutions in the world, for providing specialised financial services. Each institution is being line-tuned for a specific market, while offering the entire HDFC customer base the highest standards of quality in product design, facilities and service.

Individual

HDFC has instituted well-defined service standards for both

depositors and deposit agents. HDFC has been able to mobilise deposits from over 8 lac depositors. Outstanding deposits grew from Rs 1,458 crores in March 1994 to Rs 7,840 crores in March 2005. Much of this success can be attributed to its strong bran, image, superior services, security and above all, the significant contribution made by HDFC's deposit agents. HDFC has over 50,000 deposit agents and distributes all its retail savings (deposit) products primarily through this channel.

HDFC has been awarded "AAA" rating for its deposits from both CRISIL and ICRA for the ELEVENTH consecutive year, representing highest safety as regards timely payment of principal and interest.

Benefits of an HDFC Individual Deposit:

1. Highest Safety
2. Tax Benefits
3. Attractive Returns
4. Quick Loan Facility
5. Nomination Facility
6. Demand Draft Facility
7. High Service Standards
8. Electronic Clearing Service

- **Highest Safety:** 'FAAA' and 'MAAA' rating affirmed for the eleventh consecutive year by CRISIL and ICRA respectively.
- **Tax Benefits:** TDS: No tax deduction at source on interest from deposits upto Rs 5,000 per branch in a Financial Year.
- **Attractive Returns:** HDFC deposits are Available throughout the year and offer Attractive, Assured returns to investors. Interest rates offered are higher than that offered by most of the commercial banks.
- **Quick Loan Facility:** Loan against deposit is available after 3 months from the date of deposit upto 75% of the deposit amount subject to the other terms and conditions framed by

HDFC. Interest on such loans will be 2% above the deposit rate. This facility is not available for Easyway Savings and deposits from minors.

- **Nomination Facility:** Individual depositors, singly or jointly, can nominate under this facility. In case the deposit is placed in the name of a minor the nomination can be made only by a person lawfully entitled to act on behalf of the minor. Power of attorney holder or any person acting in representative capacity as holder of an office or otherwise cannot nominate. The nominee shall have the right to receive die amount due in respect of deposit on death of all the depositors and payment by HDFC to the nominee shall constitute foil discharge to HDFC of its liability in respect of the deposit.
- **Demand Draft Facility:** Outstation depositors can send demand drafts after deducting demand draft charges. This facility is not available to investors under Easyway Savings. This facility is applicable for places where HDFC does not have an office.
- **High Servicc Standards:** Depositors are offered across the counter services for new deposits, renewals, repayments and loan against deposit facility. Further, all enquiries through email, post, telephone and in person are attended to immediately.
- **Electronic Clearing Service:** This facility is provided to depositor's in select centres whereby the interest will be credited directly to the depositors' bank account. The depositor would receive a credit entry "ECS HDFC" in his passbook/bank statement. Intimation of interest credited would be sent on an annual basis. Your bank will not levy any charge for MIS facility as per present RBI guidelines. Presently MIS facility is being offered by us at the following centers.
- **ECS Centres:** Ahmedabad, Bangalore, Bhubaneshwar, Kolkata, Chandigarh, Chennai, Hyderabad, Jaipur, Kanpur, Mumbai, Nagpur, Nasik, New Delhi, Pune and Vadodara.

Housing Finance Sector

Against the milieu of rapid urbanisation and a changing socioeconomic scenario, the demand for housing has grown explosively. The importance of the housing sector in the economy can be illustrated by a few key statistics. According to the National Building Organisation (NBO), the total demand for housing is estimated at 2 million units per year and the total housing shortfall is estimated to be 19.4 million units, of which 12.76 million units is from rural areas and 6.64 million units from urban areas. The housing industry is the second largest employment generator in the country. It is estimated that the budgeted 2 million units would lead to the creation of an additional 10 million man-years of direct employment and another 15 million man-years of indirect employment.

Having identified housing as a priority area in the Ninth Five Year Plan (1997-2002), the National Housing Policy has envisaged an investment target of Rs 1,500 billion for tills sector. In order to achieve this investment target, the Government needs to make low cost funds easily available and enforce legal and regulatory reforms.

Product and Services offered by HDFC Bank

The following tables summarises the products and services and customer segments offered by HDFC Bank:

Table 1: Personal banking

Loan Product		Deposit Product		Investment & Insurance	
•	Auto Loan	•	Saving a/c	•	Mutual Fund
•	Loan Against Security	•	Current a/c	•	Bonds
•	Loan Against Property	•	Fixed deposit	•	Knowledge Centre
•	Personal loan	•	Demat a/c	•	Insurance
•	Credit card	•	Safe Deposit	•	General and Health
• • •	2-wheeler loan Commercial vehicles finance	•	Lockers	 • •	Insurance Equity and Derivatives Mudra Gold Bar
•	Home loans				

(*Contd...*)

•	Retail business				
•	banking				
•	Tractor loan				
•	Working Capital				
•	Finance				
•	Construction				
•	Equipment Finance				
•	Health Care Finance				
•	Education Loan				
•	Gold Loan				
	Cards		**Payment Services**		**Access To Bank**
•	Credit Card	•	Net Safe	•	Net Banking
•	Debit Card	•	Merchant	•	One View
•	Prepaid Card	•	Prepaid Refill	•	Insta Alert
	Forex Services	•	Bill Pay		Mobile Banking
•	Product & Services	•	Visa Bill pay	•	ATM
•	Trade Services	•	Insta Pay	•	PhoneBanking
• •	Forex service Branch Locater RBI Guidelines	• • •	Direct Pay Visa Money Transfer e–Monies	• •	Email Statements Branch Network
		•	Electronic Funds Transfer		
		•	Online Payment of Direct		
			Tax		

Table 2: Wholesale banking

Corporate	Small and Medium Enterprises	Government Sector	Financial Institutions and Trusts
Large Corporates	• Funded Services	• Tax Collection	• Financial Institution
• Funded Services	• Non Funded Services	• E-Ticketing	• Mutual Funds
• Non Funded Services	• Specialized Services	• Booking of L/C's	• Stock Brokers
• Value Added Services	• Value added Services	• Collection of Stamp duty	• Insurance Companies
• Internet Banking	• Internet Banking	• Disbursement of Pension	• Commodities Business

(Contd...)

Supply Chain Partners		• Electronic Collection of Fees	• Trusts
• Dealer Financing		• Collection of Property Tax	
• Vendor Financing			
• Agricultural Lending			

Table 3: NRI services

	Accounts & Deposits		**Remittances**
•	Rupee Saving a/c	•	North America
•	Rupee Current a/c	•	UK
•	Rupee Fixed Deposits	•	Europe
•	Foreign Currency Deposits	•	South East Asia
•	Accounts for Returning Indians	•	Middle East
		•	Africa
		•	Others
		•	Quick remit
		•	India Link
		•	Cheque Lock Box
		•	Telegraphic/ Wire Transfer
		•	Funds Transfer Cheques/DDs/TCs
Investment & Insurances		**Loans**	
•	Mutual Funds	•	Home Loans
•	Private Banking	•	Loans Against Securities
•	Portfolio Investment Scheme	•	Loans Against Deposits
		•	Gold Credit Card
Payment Services		**Access To Bank**	
•	Net Safe	•	Net Banking
•	Bill Pay	•	One View
•	Insta Pay	•	Insta Alert
•	Direct Pay	•	ATM
•	Visa Money	•	Phone Banking
•	Online Donation	•	Email Statements
		•	Branch Network

Transactional Banking Services of HDFC Bank

HDFC bank offers a wide range of commercial and transactional banking services and treasury products to wholesale and retail customers. The bank has three key business segments:

1. **Wholesale Banking Services:** The bank's target market ranges from large, blue-chip manufacturing companies in

the Indian corporate to small and mid-sized corporates and agri-based businesses. For these customers, the Bank provides a wide range of commercial and transactional banking services, including working capital finance, trade services, transactional services, cash management, etc. The bank is also a leading provider of structured solutions, which combine cash management services with vendor and distributor finance for facilitating superior supply chain management for its corporate customers. Based on its superior product deliver/service levels and strong customer orientation, the Bank has made significant inroads into the banking consortia of a number of leading Indian corporates including multinationals, companies from the domestic business houses and prime public sector companies. It is recognised as a leading provider of cash management and transactional banking solutions to corporate customers, mutual funds, stock exchange members and banks.

2. **Retail Banking Services:** The objective of the Retail Bank is to provide its target market customers a full range of financial products and banking services, giving the customer a one stop window for all his/her banking requirements. The products are backed by world-class service and delivered to customers through the growing branch network, as well as through alternative delivery channels like ATMs, Phone Banking, Net Banking and Mobile Banking.

   The HDFC Bank preferred programme for high net worth individuals, the HDFC Bank Plus and the Investment Advisory Services programmes have been designed keeping in mind needs of customers who seek distinct financial solutions, information and advice on various investment avenues. The Bank also has a wide array of retail loan products including Auto Loans, Loans against marketable securities, Personal Loans and Loans for Two-wheelers. It is also leading provider of Depository Participant (DP) services for retail customers, providing customers the facility to hold their investments in electronic form.

HDFC Bank was the first bank in India to launch an International Debit Card in association with VISA (VISA Electron) and issues the Mastercard Maestro debit card as well. The Bank launched its credit card business in late. By March 2010, the bank had a total card base (debit and credit cards) of over 14 million. The Bank is also one of the leading players in the "merchant acquiring" business with over 90,000 Point-of-Sale (POS) terminals for debit/credit cards acceptance at merchant establishments. The Bank is well positioned as a leader in various net based B2C opportunities including a wide range of internet banking services for Fixed Deposits, Loans, Bill Payments, etc.

3. **Treasury:** Within this business, the bank has three main product areas - Foreign Exchange and Derivatives, Local Currency Money Market and Debt Securities, and Equities. With the liberalisation of the financial markets in India, corporate need more sophisticated risk management information, advice and product structures. These and fine pricing on various treasury products are provided through the bank's Treasury team. To comply with statutory reserve requirements, the bank is required to hold 25% of its deposits in government securities. The Treasury business is responsible for managing the returns and market risk on this investment portfolio.

Features and Benefits

- Dedicated Relationship Manager
- Customised Investment Solutions
- Investment Options
- Wealth Management Programme
- E-Broking
- Expedite Tax Payments
- Relationship Pricing
- On-demand exclusive privileges
- Annual Service Charge Waiver

Dedicated Relationship Manager

Your personal relationship manager is just a phone call away. These experienced and professionally trained individuals will cater to all your banking and financial services needs. So, whether it is expert advice that you seek on mutual funds or the urgency of having a demand draft issued, just ask and trust your Relationship Manager to get the job done promptly and efficiently.

Customised Investment Solutions

Comprehensive Wealth Management solutions ranging from tax efficiently investment avenues, buying and selling shares to convenient tax payment options - etc it all under one roof.

Investment Options

Choose from a wide range of Mutual Funds, RBI Relief Bonds, Insurance and other tax effective investment avenues like infrastructure Bonds (NHAI bonds, Electrification Bonds and so on). We assure you that you will find a product that suits your need, but in high return, quick liquidity or capital preservation.

Wealth Management Programme

Benefit from extensive research across Equities, Derivatives, Debt and Mutual Funds in addition to a dedicated Advisor to take care of your financial needs. Keeping your risk profile in mind, we will customise an investment strategy for you, restructure your portfolio and allocate your assets wisely in order to realise your long term investment goals.

E-Broking

HDFC Bank offers a gateway for e-Broking, via HDFC Securities Trading Account, to facilitate easy T+2 settlements at a special price. Enjoy the convenience and flexibility of buying and selling shares over the phone or the internet. Link your Saving Bank account and Demat Account to the Securities Trading Account, thus allowing seamless flow of funds and shares between accounts. Being a preferred customer enables you to open free multiple Demat Accounts.

Expedite Tax Payments

Step into the nearest authorised branch and pay your taxes by cash or through HDFC Bank cheque and collect your challan immediately over the counter.

Relationship Pricing

Get preferential pricing across a wide range of products like Auto Loans, Personal Loans, Home Loans and Loans against Securities. Buy a Mudra Gold Bar at a 5% discount, get a free Demat Account with discounted rates on transactions, and may more such privileges.

On demand exclusive privileges

- Get Free alerts on your mobile phone or in your mailbox by registering for your Insta-Alert Facility. It comes at no cost to you.
- Profit and E-Banking Services of HDFC.
- Register for free a-Age Banking - through Mobile- Banking, Net-Banking or 24-hour Phone-Banking facilities.
- You do not need to keep a minimum account balance in your accounts.
- Free preferred International Gold Debit Card, with higher spending limit of up to Rs 50,000 and cash withdrawal of up to Rs 25.000 in a single day. International Titanium Card or International Gold Credit Card.
- Free International Titanium Card or International Gold Credit Card, with value added features.
- Request for a free "At Par" cheque book payable at any HDFC Bank branch across the country, doing away with the need for asking for a demand draft.
- Avail of a locker at just 50% of the annual free.
- You can have cash of up to Rs 1,00,000 delivered at your doorstep (currently available only in Delhi, Chennai, Kolkata

and Mumbai). Avail of this facility twice a month free of charge.

- Preferential Forex Rates.
- Avail of combined monthly statement of Savings, Current and Fixed Deposit accounts you hold with yours as the first name.
- Free Standing Instructions facility.
- We arrange to pick up cheques and other instructions (excluding cash) from your residence.
- Avail of the Bill-Pay facility and take care of all your utility bills and LIC premiums through Phone-Banking and Net-Banking.
- We also cater to the needs of your business - for a Loan Against Property or a Business Loan, Trade Finance or a Commercial Vehicle Loan, any many more, just call your Relationship Manager and relax.
- Profit and E-Banking Services of HDFC.

Annual Service Charge Waiver

As a Preferred Customer you are entitled to a waiver of up to per annum on a host of service charges like:

- Demand Draft / Manager's Cheques Charges.
- Inter-branch funds transfer charges.
- Stop payment charges.
- Cheque return / collection charge.
- DD Cancellation charges.
- Hold Mail charges.
- Duplicate statement charges.
- Certificate of Balance charges.
- FIRC charges.
- Recovery of old records charges.

E-Banking Concept of HDFC Bank

HDFC Bank offers a comprehensive range of transactions across multiple products through its net banking channel so just login to net banking and conduct **175+transactions** from the comfort of your home or office.You can check your account balance, book fixed and recurring deposits, download account statement upto five years, pay your bills, recharge your mobile/DTH connection and much more in a secure environment.

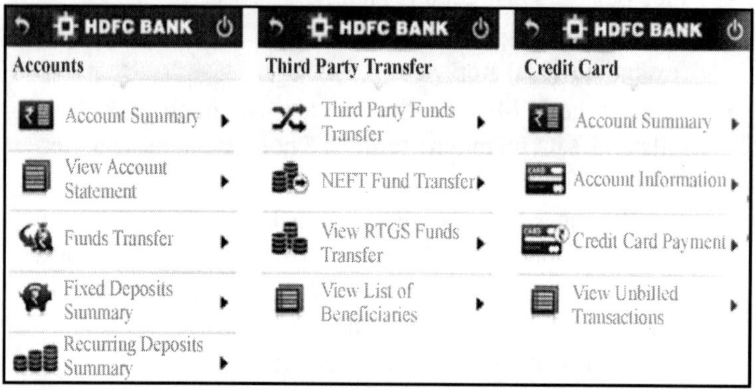

Figure 13 : E-Banking Services of HDFC.

HDFC E-Banking Services

Net Banking is an incredibly convenient and powerful tool, letting you do everything you want with your accounts at the click of a mouse. It is real time, giving up –to –the –Second details on your account. Some of the transactions you can do through net banking are:-

- Check your account balances and download five years account statement in five formats instantly.
- Book fixed deposit/recurring deposit.
- Pay Utility Bills.
- View your credit card detail and pay your credit card bills.
- Recharge your prepaid mobile and DTH connections.
- Invest in mutual funds online.
- Book IRCTC tickets online.
- Purchase a gift card.

- Pay your taxes online.
- Update your PAN details online.
- View your tax credit statements (Form 26 AS).
- Request for a demand draft/cheque book.
- Request stock payment for a cheque/hot list your debit card/ credit card.
- View your loan details.
- Apply for IPO.
- Request for a Debit Card pin registration.
- Register for third party transfer.
- Transfer funds between accounts within HDFC bank and others banks accounts.

How to Register For Net-Banking

Net-Banking registration is given by default to all HDFC Bank customer. In case you are not register for net banking, it is quick and easy.

There are many ways through which you can register are:-

1. **Online:-**
   - Resident customers and Non Resident customers with domestic mobile no. registered with the bank, can register for net-banking online by following the below steps.
   - Enter your customer ID and confirm your mobile no.
   - Input the **One time password** which you have received on your mobile no.
   - Select your debit card and input the debit card details.
   - Select your **IPIN.**
   - Login to net-banking using the newly set **IPIN.**
2. **ATM:-**
   - Visit your nearest HDFC Bank ATM.
   - Enter your HDFC Bank Debit Card No. and your ATM PIN.
   - Select "other option" from the main screen.

- Select "Net-Banking Registration" and confirm.
- We will courier the **IPIN** to your mailing address.

3. **Phone Banking:-**
   - Call the phone banking no. in your city and give your customer ID and Telephone Identification No. (TIN) or Debit Card PIN.
   - Our phone banking agent will take your net-banking registration request.
   - We will call you're the IPIN to your mailing address in our records within 5 days.
4. **Branch:-**
   - Download the net-banking registration form.
   - Fill the form and submit it your nearest HDFC Bank Branch.
   - We will courier the IPIN to your mailing address in our records.
   - Profit and E-Banking Services of HDFC.

HDFC BANK
We understand your world

Application form for NetBanking (Authorised Signatories of Trust/Firm/Corporate)

Details of Trust/Firm/Corporate

Name of Trust/Firm/Corporate :

Customer ID No. :

Declaration

I have read and understood the Terms and Conditions (a copy of which I am in possession of) relating to opening of an account and various services including but not limited to NetBanking facility. I accept and agree to be bound by the said Terms and Conditions including those excluding/limiting the Bank's liability. I understand that in the event of my already being registered for Netbanking, this application will be treated as an authenticated request for regeneration of my IPIN I agree that the Bank may debit my account for service charges as applicable for time to time.

Authorised Signatory Details

1. Customer ID No. :

 Customer Name :
 First Name Middle Name Last Name

 Email ID :

 Signature : ____________ Date : ____________

2. Customer ID No. :

 Customer Name :
 First Name Middle Name Last Name

 Email ID :

 Signature : ____________ Date : ____________

3. Customer ID No. :

 Customer Name :
 First Name Middle Name Last Name

 Email ID :

 Signature : ____________ Date : ____________

4. Customer ID No. :

 Customer Name :
 First Name Middle Name Last Name

 Email ID :

 Signature : ____________ Date : ____________

5. Customer ID No. :

Customer Name :
First Name Middle Name Last Name

Email ID :

Signature : Date :

6. Customer ID No. :

Customer Name :
First Name Middle Name Last Name

Email ID :

Signature : Date :

7. Customer ID No. :

Customer Name :
First Name Middle Name Last Name

Email ID :

Signature : Date :

8. Customer ID No. :

Customer Name :
First Name Middle Name Last Name

Email ID :

Signature : Date :

For Bank use only

Branch :

Signature verified by :

Account No. verified by :

Date NetBanking password generated :

C114 / V2.0 / 13.12.06 / P0330

REFERENCES

1. Accenture, (2007). "Global Customer Satisfaction Survey: Customer Satisfaction in the Changing Global Economy", www.customerservice. com.
2. Amuthan, R; (2004). "A Study on Retail Banking Strategies in Private Sector Banks with Special Reference to HDFC Bank and I.C.I.C.I. Bank Ltd", Journal of Indian Marketing, pp. 31-34.
3. Banking on Customer Satisfaction (2007). www.bankingstrategies.com 4. Bhatia, Gaurav, "Customer Satisfaction Survey", www.mphasis.com
5. "Customers' Satisfaction: Improving Quality and Access to Services and Support in Vulnerable Neighbourhoods," www.customerservice. com
6. Kumar, Manoj (2004). "A Comparative study of customer service", A Project Report.
7. List of banks in India; www.banknetindia.co.in
8. Parimal, Vyas. "Customer satisfaction: As core competence", Indian Journal of Marketing, pp. 16-17.
9. Sinvakumar, V. J. (2005). "Building Sustainable Competitive Strength in Indian Banking Industry-The Role of KCRM," International Conference on Services Management, pp. 779-86.
10. Thomas, E. DeCarlo, and Thomas, W. Leigh (1996). "Impact of Salesperson Attraction on Sales Managers' Attributions and Feedback," Journal of Marketing, Vol. 60, pp. 47-49.
11. Valarie, A. Zeithaml, Leonard, L. Beery, and Parasuraman, (1996). "The Behavioral Consequences of Service Quality," Journal of Marketing, Vol. 60. pp. 31-46.

Chapter - VII

Profile and E-banking Services of ICICI

Bank Profile

ICICI Bank Ltd. is India's second largest financial services company headquartered in Mumbai, India. It offers a wide range of banking products and financial services to corporate and retail customers through a variety of delivery channels and through its specialised subsidiaries in the areas of investment banking, life and non-life insurance, venture capital and asset management. The Bank has a network of 2,533 branches and 6,800 ATMs in India, and has a presence in 19 countries, including India. The bank has subsidiaries in the United Kingdom, Russia, and Canada; Branches in United States, Singapore, Bahrain, Hong Kong, Sri Lanka, Qatar and Dubai International Finance Centre; and representative offices in United Arab Emirates, China, South Africa, Bangladesh, Thailand, Malaysia and Indonesia. ICICI Bank was established in 1994 by the Industrial Credit and Investment Corporation of India, an Indian financial institution, as a wholly owned subsidiary. The parent company was formed in 1955 as a joint-venture of the World Bank, India's public sector banks and public-sector insurance companies to provide project financing to Indian industry. The bank was initially known as the Industrial Credit and Investment Corporation of India Bank, before it changed its name to the abbreviated ICICI Bank. The parent company was later merged into ICICI Bank.

History of ICICI Bank

ICICI Bank is India's second-largest bank with total assets of about Rs 1 trillion and a network of about 540 branches and offices and over 1,000 ATMs. ICICI Bank offers a wide range of banking products and financial services to corporate and retail customers through a variety of delivery channels and through its specialised subsidiaries and affiliates in the areas of investment banking and information technology. ICICI Bank's equity shares are listed in India on stock exchanges at Chennai, Muzaffarnagar, Kolkata and Vadodara, the Stock Exchange, Mumbai and the National Stock Exchange of India Limited and its American Depositary Receipts (ADRs) are listed on the New York Stock Exchange (NYSE).

ICICI Bank was originally promoted in 1994 by ICICI Limited, as an Indian financial institution, and was its wholly owned subsidiary. ICICI's shareholding in ICICI Bank was reduced to 46% through a public offering of shares in India in fiscal year 1998, an equity offering in the form of ADRs listed on the NYSE in fiscal year 2000, ICICI Bank's acquisition of Bank of Madura Limited in an all-stock amalgamation in fiscal year 2001, and secondary market sales by ICICI to institutional investors in fiscal year 2001 and fiscal year 2002. ICICI was formed in 1955 at the initiative of the World Bank, the Government of India and representatives of Indian industry. The principal objective was to create a development financial institution for providing medium-term and long-term project financing to Indian businesses. In the 1990s, ICICI transformed its business from a development financial institution offering only project finance to a diversified financial services group offering a wide variety of products and services, both directly and through a number of subsidiaries and affiliates like ICICI Bank. In 1999, ICICI become the first Indian company and the first bank or financial institution from non-Japan Asia to be listed on the NYSE.

After consideration of various corporate structuring alternatives in the context of the emerging competitive scenario in the Indian banking industry, and the move towards universal banking, the managements of ICICI and ICICI Bank formed the view that the merger of ICICI with ICICI Bank would be the optimal strategic alternative for both entities, and would create the optimal legal structure for the ICICI group's universal banking strategy. The merger would enhance value for ICICI shareholders through the merged entity's access to low-cost deposits, greater opportunities for earning fee-based income and the ability to participate in the payments system and provide transaction-banking services. The merger would enhance value for ICICI Bank shareholders through a large capital base and scale of operations, seamless access to ICICI's strong corporate relationships built up over five decades, entry into new business segments, higher market share in various business segments, particularly fee-based services, and access to the vast talent pool of ICICI and its subsidiaries. In October 2001, the Boards of Directors of ICICI and ICICI Bank approved the merger of ICICI and two of its wholly owned retail finances subsidiaries, ICICI Personal Financial Services Limited and ICICI Capital Services Limited, with ICICI Bank. The merger was approved by shareholders of ICICI and ICICI Bank in January 2002, by the High Court of Gujarat at Ahmedabad in March 2002, and by the High Court of Judicature at Mumbai and the Reserve Bank of India in April 2002. Consequent to the merger, the ICICI group's financing and banking operations, both wholesale and retail, have been integrated in a single entity. ICICI Bank has signed an agreement to use the NCR switch mark technology for online-networking of all its ATMs, the officials said they network would come into place in September.

ICICI Bank recently restructured its organisational structure by setting up strategic business units for retail banking, corporate banking and treasury operations, as independent profit centers. ICICI is all set to launch a 60- second television commercial on August 15, 1999.

In 2000, ICICI Bank became the first Indian bank to list on the New York Stock Exchange with its $175-million American depository shares issue generating a demand book 13 times its size at $2.2 billion.

The Bank proposes to bring credit cards to the large, underserved population in rural and semi-urban areas. Sky Cell Communications Ltd, one of the two cellular service providers in Chennai, has launched 'Sky Banking', for which the company has tied up with ICICI Bank and HDFC Bank. The ICICI has announced the launch of mobile banking services for its customers, using the wireless application protocol (WAP) technology.

Ford India has tied up with ICICI Bank to introduce a scheme, enabling nonresident Indians (NRIs) to purchase a Ford Ikon car for their friends and relatives in India. ICICI Bank has set up an ATM facility at an Indian Oil Corporation petro-diesel outlet at Chennai.

ICICI Bank has tied up with Chennai Telephones to provide Internet bill payment facility to its customers.

After State Bank of India, which is unarguably the most widely used bank in India, both ICICI and HDFC banks are amongst the top Indian banks in terms of customer base, infrastructure and facilities provided and both have fairly succeeded in providing powerful Net-banking services.

ICICI Bank Names Consultant for Government Business

ICICI Bank has appointed international consultancy major monitor group to help the bank in identification of business prospects in the government sector which has recently been identifies as a focus area.

Monitor will help ICICI get business from the government sector, particularly the infrastructure sector mandates. The bank did not consider government business a focus area till sometime back. Now, Monitor Group will study investment prospect of tourism in Rajasthan, opportunities for the government of Andhra Pradesh and investment prospects for the bank through the government in cities such as Pune and Kolkata.

"We are trying to find out how ICICI Bank can be a partner to the government in development plans and projects. The bank has initiated fresh focus towards the government which is a major source of business and we would like to increase relationship with government agencies," ICICI officials said.

Monitor Group will find out ways and means for ICICI Bank through which the latter "Can solve government fund flow problems and how ICICI Bank can play a role in the projects," bank officials said.

This is a test study and if there is a positive response from the government then more such specific developmental studies will be taken up by the bank as partners to development.- Economics Times

Product and Services Offered by ICICI Bank

ICICI Bank offers wide variety of Deposit Products to suit your requirements. Coupled with convenience of networked branches / ATMs and facility of E-channels like Internet and Mobile Banking, ICICI Bank brings banking at your doorstep. Select any of our deposit products and provide your details online and our representative will contact you for Account Opening.

ICICI Bank offers you a power packed Savings Account with a host of convenient features and banking channels to transact through. So now you can bank at your convenience, without the stress of waiting in queues.

Senior Citizen Services

We understand that as you reach the age to retire, you do have certain concerns:

1. whether your hard earned money is safe and secure
2. whether your investments give you the kind of returns that you need.

That's why we have an ideal Banking Service for those who are 60 years and above. The Senior Citizen Services from ICICI Bank has several advantages that are tailored to bring more convenience and enjoyment in your life.

Young Stars

It's really important to help children learn the value of finances and money management at an early age. Banking is a serious business, but we make banking a pleasure and at the same time children learn how to manage their personal finances.

Fixed Deposits

Safety, Flexibility, Liquidity and Returns!!!! A combination of unbeatable features of the Fixed Deposit from ICICI Bank.

Recurring Deposit

When expenses are high, you may not have adequate funds to make big investments. But simply going ahead without saving for the future is not an option for you. Through ICICI Bank Recurring Deposit you can invest small amounts of money every month that ends up with a large saving on maturity. So you enjoy twin advantages- affordability and higher earnings.

Documentation

Applicants must satisfy the following documentation requirements:

- Identity proof
- Proof of communication address
- Self cheque (if the applicant is not visiting the branch for account opening)

Identity Proof (Any one of the following)	Proof of communication address (Any one of the following)
Original letter of introduction from existing bank along with KYC cheque of the same Bank	Introduction by an existing and satisfactory customer as address proof
Driving License – Book type or laminated & embossed	Latest Electricity Bill
Voter Identity Card with KYC cheque for operating accounts. Cash can be accepted for Term deposits.	Certificate from the postal office confirming address of applicant
Employee Identity Card	Original Letter from Employer certifying the residential address of applicant. Signature of the employee has to be attested on the letter.
PAN Card	Telephone bills from any telephone service providers and mobile service providers (KYC cheque mandatory for mobile service providers)
Defence Dependent's card	Consumer gas connection card/book/ Pipe Gas bill (same as electricity bill)
Ex-Service Man Card	Certificate from the ward/equivalent rank officer, maintaining election roll, certifying address of the applicant

(*Contd...*)

Bar Council/Indian Medical Association Card/Senior Citizen Card	Registered and valid Lease/ Leave agreement with copies of utility bills
PIO Booklet for returning NRIs	Post Office Savings Pass Book with KYC cheque
MAPIN card	Statement of account or Pass Book of a scheduled commercial bank with entries of at least last 3 months alongwith KYC cheque
	Premium Receipt from any Banking company
	Certificate by Village Extension Officer (VEO)/Village Head or equal rank officers
	Domicile Certificate with communication address and Photograph

Features

- The ICICI Bank Ncash debit card is a debit-cum-ATM card providing you with the convenience of acceptance at merchant establishments and cash withdrawals at ATMs.
- Free Access to any Bank's ATM – The next time you want to withdraw cash from your ICICI Bank account, just walk into any bank's ATM and use your ICICI Bank ATM-cum-Debit card for as many as 9 free transactions (including cash withdrawal and balance enquiry) in a quarter. This offer is available to customers who maintain more than Rs 25,000 in a given quarter in their domestic Savings Account with ICICI Bank. The above benefit can be availed in the next quarter.
- Anywhere Banking - This facility entitles the account holder to withdraw or deposit cash upto a limit of Rs 50,000 across all ICICI Bank branches.
- You can give us various types of standing instructions like transferring to fixed deposit accounts at regular intervals.
- An average quarterly balance of Rs 5,000 only.

Minimum Balance

Type of Account	Balance
Savings Account	Rs 5,200

Non-maintenance of the minimum average quarterly balance attracts a fee of Rs 750 per quarter.

Nomination

- The facility of Nomination is available for relationships in the names of individuals. Unless otherwise specifically, given in writing by depositors, nomination in deposit accounts will be at Customer ID level.
- A depositor(s) however has / have the right to specify different nominations at account level by completing the appropriate forms.
- Further, the applicant(s) is / are at liberty to change the nominee during the currency of the relationship accounts with the Bank through declaration to that effect in the appropriate form.

A. Repatriable: Repatriable funds (i.e. those which can be taken abroad) need to be kept in a separate bank account, i.e. NRE Bank account. Typically, funds brought in from abroad are permitted in such an account. Investments made from such funds can be repatriated, i.e. proceeds from sale or otherwise from such investments can be taken abroad. Such investments are maintained in a Repatriable Demat account.

B. Non-repatriable: Non-repatriable funds (i.e. those which cannot be taken abroad) need to be kept separate from repatriable funds in a separate bank account i.e. NRO Bank account. Investments made from such funds cannot be repatriated, i.e. proceeds from sale or otherwise from such investments cannot be taken abroad. Such investments are maintained in a Non-Repatriable Demat account. Money once transferred from NRE account to NRO account loses its repatriability and hence, cannot be transferred back to NRE account.

Mode of Investment

A. Portfolio Investment Scheme (PINS): Portfolio Investment Scheme (PINS) is a scheme of the Reserve Bank of India (RBI) under which the 'Non Resident Indians (NRIs)' and 'Person of Indian Origin (PIO's), can purchase and sell shares and convertible debentures of Indian Companies on a recognised stock exchange in India by routing all such purchase/sale transactions through their account held with a Designated Bank Branch. The Designated Bank maintains a record of all investments done under PINS (PINS portfolio).

B. Non - PINS: Any investment other than under PINS is Typically, this includes:

1. Subscription to Primary market offerings (IPOs)
2. Investments made when resident in India.
3. Investments in Mutual funds
4. Investments in derivatives
5. Gifts and Inheritance

Deciding Combination

You may have to open demat accounts of a specific combination if you already hold physical shares in that combination. The physical shares can be converted into electronic form in your demat account by submitting the certificates along with a demat request form. You should also open the required combination under the correct type of demat account:

PINS NRE: For shares acquired earlier under PINS on repatriation basis.

PINS NRO: For shares acquired earlier under PINS on non-repatriation basis.

Non-PINS NRE: For shares acquired earlier other than under PINS on repatriation basis.

Non-PINS NRO: For shares acquired earlier other than under PINS on non-repatriation basis and also when 'Resident' in India.

I. **Terms and Conditions for establishing relationship and Operating Accounts** (For Resident Individuals)

1. **Establishing a Relationship**

   - Applicant(s) desiring to open a Relationship need(s) to sign a Relationship form and declare therein that he/she/they has/have agreed to abide by the rules which are in force from time to time.
   - Applicant is required to furnish Identity Proof and Address proof as follows while establishing a banking relationship with the Bank:

Identity Proof

- Verified true copy of valid passport
- Letter from existing bank
- Valid driving license
- Valid employee identity card
- Valid PAN card
- Valid photo credit card along with the current billing cycle (latest) statement
- True copy of valid arms license issued by Govt of India/ State govts/Union territory with photograph
- Valid pension book
- Valid freedom fighter's pass issued by Home Ministry of Government of India

E-Banking Concept

E-Banking is the convenient way to do banking from the comfort of your home or office. Avoid the queue or delays and try ICICI simple and secure Internet banking facility for an unmatched online banking experience. Millions of ICICI bank customers are using internet banking to:-

- Checking account statement.
- Transfer funds.
- Open a fixed deposit account.

- Pay utility bills.
- Recharge prepaid mobile/DTH.

Figure 14 : ICICI E-Banking Services.

E-Banking Services

E-Banking offers a host of services and facilities that give you real time access to your account. You can make or receive payments to ICICI Bank account and Non ICICI Bank accounts, open fixed and recurring deposits, view account details, request a cheque book and a lot more, while you are online:-

1. **Fund Transfer:** With **ICICI Bank.com**, transferring funds from your ICICI bank account is very simple and convenient. There are various option provided online for transferring funds. You can transfer funds to:-
    - Your own ICICI bank account.
    - Other ICICI bank account.
    - Non ICICI bank account using NEFT.
    - Non ICICI bank account using RTGS.
    - Other account using IMPS. (24*7)
    - Profile and E-Banking Services of ICICI

2. **Bill Payment:** Pay bills from the comfort of your home and office. This is a facility idle for your electricity, telephone, mobile and other bills. Do away with cheques with late payments and lost bills, and enjoy the convenience. You can also pay your bill without registering a payee with **ICICI QUICK PAY.**
3. **Online Mobile Recharge:** Now you are no longer need to rush to the vendor for buying pre paid mobile recharge codes, every time your talk time runs out. Just top-up your prepaid mobile cards by loging into internet banking on **ICICI Bank.com** and this online mobile recharge service is absolutely free for all ICICI bank account holders.
4. **Pay any Visa Credit Card:** Pay any Visa credit card is a revolutionary service that allows you to transfer money from your bank account to any other visa credit card anytime, anywhere in India.
   - Forget cumbersome and time consuming demand drafts, cheques and pay orders.
   - Transact from the comfort of your home or office through ICICI bank internet banking.
   - Send money to over 27 million visa card holders across 150 cities in India.
   - Send money to any visa credit card issued in India.
5. **Invest Online:** ICICI efforts towards making investments more convenient. An online service offered to all resident Indians having an ICICI saving account that will enable you to transact online.
   - Purchase, redeem or switch securities online.
   - Systematic investment facility (SIP) is available online.
   - NAV and Mutual funds, Portfolio can be tracked easily.
   - Profile and E-Banking Services of ICICI
6. **Insure online:** ICICI work hard to provide the best to our families. So that they lead happy and comfortable lives. Certain events like unfortunate death of earning member,

ICICI E-Banking Application Form

Application for Internet Banking, Phone Banking and Mobile Banking

(All fields with * are mandatory to be filled.)

Name of the applicant: Mr./Ms./Mrs. ______________ ______________ ______________

Surname * First Name * Middle Name *

Mailing address : Address * ______________________________________

____

City * : ______________ Pin Code * : ☐☐☐☐☐☐

Email Address * : ______________@______________ Phone No. ______________

Mobile No. : ______________ Mother's Maiden Name * : ______________

Date of birth * : ____/____/____
dd mm yy

Instructions

I) In case of joint accounts, the applicant is required to obtain the attached mandate from the joint account holder(s).

II) ICICI Bank accountholders can access their bank accounts through ICICI Bank Internet Banking only where the mode of operation of ICICI Bank account is Single/Either or Survivor/Anyone or Survivor.

Please tick one of the following:

☐ I want to apply for ICICI Bank Internet Banking and/or Phone Banking and link my account(s), as mentioned below, to my User ID.

☐ I have an Internet Banking User-ID, but do not remember it and I want it to be resent to me along with password.

☐ I want to apply for ICICI Bank Mobile Banking Service in respect of my account(s), as mentioned below. I wish to subscribe to all the alerts as are displayed on the website www.icicibank.com as applicable to my account(s) mentioned below.

☐ I have Relationship number for Phone Banking, but do not remember it and I want it to be resent to me along with password.

☐ My existing Internet Banking User ID is ______________ and/or Relationship number for Phone Banking is ______________ and I want to link my account(s), as mentioned below, to it.

[Please fill account details below]

ACCOUNT DETAILS:

I confirm that I am the sole account holder or I have the required mandate from the joint account holder(s) to singly operate the accounts.

Bank A/c No./ Credit Card No./DP ID Demat A/c No./Loans against Securities A/c No.	Name of the Branch	Mode of Operation (tick one)	Service to be Subscribed (strike off the Option not to be applied)	Customer ID (For official use only)
		* Single * Joint	Internet/ Mobile/ Phone Banking	
		* Single * Joint	Internet/ Mobile/ Phone Banking	

		* Single * Joint	Internet/ Mobile/ Phone Banking	

Declaration:

I affirm, confirm and undertake that I have read and understood the Terms and Conditions for usage of the Internet Banking, Phone Banking and/or Mobile Banking service of ICICI Bank Limited and I am aware of Charges Applicable for the Mobile Banking Service, as set forth in www.icicibank.com, and that I agree on my own behalf, or as the mandate holder on behalf of the joint account holders, and will adhere to all the terms/conditions of opening/ applying/ availing/ maintaining/ operating (as applicable) for usage of the Internet Banking, Phone Banking and/or Mobile Banking service of ICICI Bank Limited as may be in force from time to time. I further authorize ICICI Bank Limited to debit my Account(s) towards any Charges for Mobile Banking Service.

I declare that all the particulars and information given in this application form (and all documents referred or provided therewith) are true, correct, complete and up-to-date in all respects and I, and other joint accountholders have not withheld any information. I understand that certain particulars given by me are required by the operational guidelines governing banking companies. I agree and undertake to provide any further information that ICICI Bank Ltd./its Group Companies may require.

I agree and understand that ICICI Bank Ltd/ Group Companies reserve the right to reject any application without providing any reason. I agree and understand that ICICI Bank Ltd/its Group Companies reserve the right to retain the application forms, and the documents provided therewith, including photographs, and will not return the same to me.

I authorize ICICI Bank Ltd./ its Group Companies or their agent to make references and enquiries which ICICI Bank Ltd/its Group Companies consider necessary in respect of or in relation to information in this application/further applications. I agree and hereby authorise ICICI Bank Ltd/its Group Companies to exchange, share or part with all the information, data or documents relating to my/our application to other ICICI Group Companies/ Banks/ Financial Institutions/ Credit Bureaus/ Agencies/ Statutory Bodies/such other persons as ICICI Bank Ltd/its Group Companies may deem necessary or appropriate as may be required for use or processing of the said information/data by such person/s or furnishing of the processed information/data/products thereof to other Banks/Financial Institutions/credit providers/users registered with such persons and shall not hold ICICI Bank Ltd/ its Group companies liable for use of this information.

I agree and understand that I have to complete further applications for specific liability products/services from ICICI Bank Ltd/its Group Companies, as prescribed from time to time, and that such further applications shall be regarded as an integral part of this application (and vice versa), and that unless otherwise disclosed in such further forms as prescribed, the particulars and information set forth herein as well as the documents referred or provided herewith are true, correct, complete and up-to-date in all respects. I agree and understand that such further applications will require incorporation of the application form number, and/or such details as ICICI Bank may prescribe, to facilitate data management

Date:__/__/__ Place __________ Signature__________
dd mm yy (Sole/First holder)

critical illness, medical emergencies, accidents can adversely affect our family's well being and finances.

ICICI Insurance plan provide you protection from life uncertainty and avenues to save for your long term financial goals. Buy ICICI Insurance product online at your convenience and secure the future of your family today.

7. **E-Locker:** ICICI E-locker is an online document storage facility to store all your valuable documents at one central secure location. Be it your birth or marriage certificate, pass book statement, life insurance policy, PAN card copy or any other prised documents, access all your documents any time conveniently.

Terms and Conditions of ICICI Net Banking

Access to Internet Banking

The User would be allotted an Internet Banking User-id and a set of secret passwords by ICICI Bank in the first instance.

- The User will be required to change the password assigned by ICICI Bank on accessing Internet Banking for the first time. As a safety measure, the User shall change the password as frequently thereafter as possible. The User acknowledges, represents and warrants that the password which will be issued to it, provides access to the Account and that User is the sole and exclusive owner and is the only authorised User of the password and accepts sole responsibility for use, confidentiality and protection of the password, as well as for all orders and information changes (i.e., change of address) entered into Accounts using such password. If the User forgets the Internet Banking password or the Internet Banking Password gets locked after a number of incorrect attempts, upto such number as may be intimated by ICICI Bank from time to time, then the User may request for the issue of a new password through the ICICI Bank 24-Hour Customer Care Centre, Internet Banking Channel or the ICICI Bank Branch and this shall not be construed as the commencement of a new contract. Such Password may be issued within such time as may be intimated by ICICI Bank from time to time. The User agrees and acknowledges that ICICI Bank shall in no way be held responsible or liable if the User incurs any loss as a result of information being disclosed by ICICI Bank regarding his Account(s) or carrying the instruction of the User pursuant to the access of the

Internet Banking and the User shall fully indemnify and hold harmless ICICI Bank and the Affiliates in respect of the same. The User shall maintain the secrecy of all information of confidential nature and shall ensure that the same is not disclosed to any person voluntarily, accidentally or by mistake. The User agrees and acknowledges that any loss, damage, liability caused or suffered by the User due to disclosure of all information of confidential nature shall be borne by the User without transferring any liability or responsibility towards ICICI Bank. The User shall comply with such guidelines, instructions or terms as ICICI Bank may prescribe from time to time with respect to the password.

- The User shall also be given a one-time facility to change the User-id to such User-id as may be suggested by ICICI Bank or as per User's own discretion. The aforesaid facility shall be available to Users only after logging in to Internet Banking, The User unconditionally undertakes to have the User-id of such number of letters/digits as may be notified by ICICI Bank at the time the User attempts to change the User-id and ensure that the same is kept confidential; and to not let any unauthorised person have access to the User's Account while the User is accessing the Internet Banking. If the User forgets the User-id or the same gets disabled after a number of incorrect password attempts, upto such number as may be intimated by ICICI Bank from time to time, then the User may request for the re-issue of his User-id through the ICICI Bank 24-Hour Customer Care Centre or the ICICI Bank Branch and this shall not be construed as the commencement of a new contract.
- In addition to User-id and password ICICI Bank may, at its discretion, advise the User to adopt such other means of authentication including but not limited to digital certification and/ or smart cards. The User shall not attempt or permit others to attempt accessing the Account information stored in the computers of ICICI Bank through any means other than the Internet Banking.

- The User shall take all necessary precautions to prevent unauthorised and illegal use of Internet Banking and unauthorised access to the Accounts provided by Internet Banking. ICICI Bank shall take all commercially reasonable care to, ensure the security of and to prevent unauthorised access to the Internet Banking using commercially reasonable technology available in India to ICICI Bank.

Liabilities of User

Neither ICICI Bank nor the Affiliate/s shall be liable for any unauthorised transactions occurring through the Internet Banking and the User hereby fully indemnifies and holds ICICI Bank and the Affiliates harmless against any action, suit, proceeding initiated against it or any loss, cost or damage incurred by it as a result thereof. ICICI Bank shall under no circumstance be held liable to the User if the Internet Banking is not available in the desired manner for reasons including but not limited to natural calamities, legal restraints, faults in the telecommunication network or network failure, or any other reason beyond the control of ICICI Bank. Under no circumstances shall ICICI Bank be liable for any damages whatsoever whether such damages are direct, indirect, incidental consequential and irrespective of whether any claim is based on loss of revenue, interruption of business or any loss of any character or nature whatsoever and whether sustained by the User or by any other person. Illegal or improper use of the Internet Banking shall render the User liable for payment of financial charges as decided by ICICI Bank or will result in suspension / termination of the Internet Banking services extended to such User/s. The aforesaid does not limit ICICI Bank's right to initiate appropriate legal proceedings against such customers.

Comparison between ICICI and HDFC E-Banking Services

The Services provided by these banks are given below:-

- Viewing of Account summary, current balance, all historic transactions, mini and detailed statements.
- Linking of your multiple accounts like Savings, Current, Credit cards, Demat, Mutual funds and Fixed deposit accounts to a single Net-banking ID.

- Transfer of funds (more on this in subsequent section).
- Requesting a new demand draft or cheque book at your address.
- Online payment of utility bills like Electricity, Gas, Landline and Mobile phone bills, Insurance premiums, Credit card bills, etc.
- Applying for new Fixed Deposits online.
- Download of Account statements in Text, Excel and MS Money formats.
- Online request for a hard copy of your bank statements at your address. ICICI charges INR 50 whereas HDFC charges INR 30 per statement request.
- Viewing status of deposited cheques or stopping the payment of a cheque.
- Both use High-grade Encryptions for secure login and transactions. ICICI uses RC4 128 bit whereas HDFC uses AES- 256 bit.
- Both have recently enabled Virtual Keyboard logins to stop any software from recording your passwords when you type them. Virtual keyboard asks you to choose the password letters by a mouse.

A closer look reveals that both these vary significantly and that ICICI Net-banking is better than HDFC Net-banking by leaps and bounds in terms of facilities.

Here is a comparison of their services feature-by-feature:

- **Transfer of Funds:** This is a major difference. ICICI Net-banking's Funds Transfer facility is much more hassle-free as compared to HDFC's Third Party Transfer (TPT) facility. The problem arises not in using the service but in applying to the service. The facility to transfer funds to yours or someone else's account, at intra or inter-bank branch, comes readily with the ICICI Net-banking subscription. That is, the facility is ready to use and you just need to add-in the new beneficiary for making the first transfer.

However, HDFC doesn't agree to this simplicity and requires you to apply to this service by filling up a hard copy of the Third Party Transfer Application Form and submitting it to any of their Bank branches or ATM. Now when we are striving for branch-less banking, this looks off-the-road to me. Moreover, user experiences say that the application is not processed promptly if you deposit the activation form at an ATM, and may cause further delays upto weeks. Hence, it is preferred to walk into the HDFC bank and talk to the representative for activation.

- **Applying for new Accounts:** You can initiate the opening of a variety of accounts online through ICICI Net-banking by submitting an online request with the details. For certain accounts like the Recurring Deposits, the request gets completed without the need for you to visit the bank, and the newly created account is accessible at your next login upon approval. On the other hand, in case for HDFC, this becomes possible only on visiting the bank branch. ICICI Net-banking also offers online self-compounding accounts like Recurring Deposits and Money Multiplier Account that HDFC Net banking doesn't.
- **Insta-Alerts Customisation:** Though both ICICI and HDFC Net-banking offers the facility of receiving message "Alerts" on your mobile to notify transactions, ICICI offers online customisation of the alerts upto the minutest details. For example you can configure the threshold amounts above which you need an alert for, and also specify whether you need the alert by an SMS or email. You can as well toggle on/off the Insta-alerts for one or more services, say if you don't want to receive the alerts for fund credits and need them only for debits. Cool, eh? Bravo ICICI.

HDFC Net-banking is also lagging behind as it doesn't allow:

- Premature liquidation of your Fixed Deposit.
- De-registration of Bill Pay facility.

whereas these are enabled by ICICI Net-banking.

Other way round: So, is there anything which is offered by HDFC Net-banking and not by ICICI Net-banking? Believe me, I had to look hard to find this and, gladly, here are some unique services that HDFC offers but ICICI doesn't:

- HDFC offers TDS Enquiry facility by which you can instantly check how much TDS (Tax Deduction at Source) was applicable on your current and previous taxable years.
- HDFC also allows re-generation of your IPIN (password) online in case you have forgotten it. However in case of ICICI, you need to call up the customer care to request a new Net-banking password and it will be delivered to you (by post) in about 5 working days.

REFERENCES

1. Krishnaveni, R. and Divya Prava, D. (2004), Measuring Service Quality in Banking Sector, *Prajnan:Journal of Social and Management Sciences,* Vol. 23, No. 1, pp. 47-55.
2. Parasuraman, A., Zeithaml, V. and Berry, L. (1988), SERVQUAL: Multiple-item Scale for Measuring Consumer Perceptions of Service Quality, *Journal of Retailing*, Vol. 64, pp. 12-40.
3. Jain, S.K. and G. Gupta (2004), Measuring Service Quality: SERVQUAL vs. SERVPERF Scales, *The Journal for Decision Makers,* Vol. 29, No. 2, pp.25-37.
4. Khalil, M.N. and J.M. Pearson (2007), The Influences of Trust on Internet Banking Acceptance, *Journal of Internet Banking and Commerce,* Vol. 12, No. 2, pp. 1-10.
5. Kothari, C.R. (2009), *Research Methodology*, Vikas Publishing House Pvt. Ltd, New Delhi.
6. Kotler, P. (2003), *Marketing Management*, Prentice Hall, New Delhi, India.
7. Valarie A. Zeithaml, A Parasuraman and Leonard L Berry (2009), Delivering Quality Service- Balancing Customer Perceptions and Expectations, Free Press, New York, US.
8. Gerrand, P. & Cunningham, J. B. (2005), The service Quality of E- Banks: An Exploratory study- *International Journal of Financial Service Management,* 1(1), pp. 102-117
9. Gupta, V, *E-Banking: Global Perspectives.* IIM Publication.
10. Johnstorn, R. (1995), The Determinants of Service Quality: Satisfiers and Dissatisfies. *International Journal of Service Industry Management,* 8(5), pp. 53-71

11. Joseph, M. McClure, C. & Joseph B. (1999), Service Quality of Banking Sector: The Impact of Technology on Service Delivery. *International Journal of Bank Marketing,* 17(4), pp. 182-191.

12. Jun, M. & Cai,S.(2001), The Key Determinants of Internet Bank Service Quality: A Content Analysis. *International Journal of Bank Marketing* 19(7), pp. 276-291.

Chapter - VIII

Data Analysis and Interpretation

Comparative Study of Performance of Selective Banks

Indian banking sector developed rapidly in the last decades. After 1991 LPG policy government has taken a various step to strengthen Indian Banking sector, among them important one was reforms in Banking Sector of India, due to this so many, private sector banks and foreign banks have entered in India with high-tech banking services. Government has also appointed various committees to strengthen Indian banking sector. Finally Basel II norms have been implemented in Indian Banking Sector.

After the liberalisation many private sector banks have started business in India. The question that we address in this study is: how effectively these banks have performed? In the past, various studies relating to financial performance of banks have been conducted by researchers. Das (2002) in his paper has made an attempt to develop an objective method for ranking the Nationalised Bank. He analyzed the performance of 17 public sector banks. Swami and Subrahmanyam (1994) has tried to study the inter-bank differences in the performance of public sector banks in India with "Taxonomic method". They found that many banks show wide disparities in their measures of performance. Technical and scale efficiency of banks study conducted by Noulas and Ketkar (2000). Bhattacharya *et. al.* (2010) and Sathye (2005) conducted to study the impact of privatisation on performance of banks. Result of both the studies was contradictory. Bhattacharya found that performance of PSB was sound as compared the private sector bank vice versa result found by Sathye in his study. Saha and Ravisanker (2000) rated 25 public sector banks using data envelopment analysis. Technical efficiency and benchmark performance of 68 commercial banks conducted by Mukheijee *et. al.* (2002). It has been found that in India, public sector banks are more efficient than both private and foreign banks. Amandeep (2000) in her study on profitability of commercial banks has attempted to examine the profits and profitability of twenty nationalised banks. She concluded that efficient management is dominant factor for profitability. Swamy (2001) studied the comparative performance of different bank groups. Das (2002) has studied the interrelationships among capital, non-performing loans and productivity of public sector, banks. Uppal (2004) conducted a comparative study of Business, Efficiency, Soundness and Productivity of New Private Sector Banks. He concluded that private sector banks are sound in urban area and has ranked the banks as per parameters. Profitability and Resource Use Efficiency in Schedule Commercial Banks in India study conducted by Qamar (2008). He found that new private sector and foreign banks are marginally more efficient than old private sector and public sector banks.

A deep examination of literature shows there are a few studies that have analyzed the e-banking performance of public and private sector banks. The present study is the addition to literature by using CAMEL method for the comparative performance of State Bank of India, PNB, ICICI Bank and HDFC Bank.

The main objective of the study is to determine the customers' satisfaction and comparison of e-banking services of PNB, SBI, ICICI and HDFC Bank. To achieve the main objective the following are set as sub-objectives:

- To study the customers' satisfaction in public sector banks
- To study the customers' satisfaction in private sector banks

To study comparative analysis of customers' satisfaction in private and public sector banks.

The following hypothesis are proposed:

(a) To be treated on public sector banks

- H1 : There exists a significant difference among the level of customers' satisfaction in the SBI and PNB.

(b) To be treated on private sector banks

- H2 : There exists a significant difference among the level of customers' satisfaction in the ICICI and HDFC Banks.

(c) To be treated on comparison

- H3 : There exists a significant difference among the level of customers' satisfaction in the public and private sector banks.

A sample of 200 respondents have been drawn from the various socio-economic strata, at different designation and having different educational qualification and belongs to different age groups on the line of convenience sampling. Four banks have been chosen for the study, two of these banks are public sector banks, namely State Bank of India and Punjab National Bank and two are private sector banks namely ICICI and HDFC Bank as follow:

Name of the banks	No of respondents
SBI	50
PNB	50
ICICI	50
HDFC	50
Total Sample Size	**200**

Primary data have been collected from a sample of 200 respondents, chosen by convenient sampling method. In order to collect the necessary data the researcher visited personally to the respondents. The questionnaire was included four variables which determine the satisfaction of the customers of selected banks regarding E-Banking services. The five points and their respective score values in the scale are given as under

Points of Scale	Assigned Score
Very Satisfied	5
Satisfied	4
Neither Satisfied Nor dissatisfied	3
Dissatisfied	2
Very Dissatisfied	1

The dimensions selected for measuring customers' satisfaction have been selected as ATM cards, fund transfer, mobile banking, net banking.

Table 4: Techniques selected are percentage, mean, standard deviation and Z-test

	Public Sector Banks				Private Sector Banks			
	SBI		PNB		HDFC		ICICI	
	Mean	St. dev.	Mean	St. dev.	Mean	St. dev.	Mean	St. dev.
ATM Cards	3.83	1.01	4.45	0.49	3.48	1.08	4.02	0.71
Fund Transfer	3.90	0.88	4.06	0.95	3.51	1.00	4.00	0.71
Mobile Banking	4.20	0.86	4.31	0.66	3.71	0.96	4.15	0.46
Net Banking	4.21	0.71	3.85	1.35	3.72	0.96	4.44	0.49
Combined Mean	4.04	0.91	4.18	0.84	3.19	1.07	2.93	0.65

Combined mean has been calculated as follows

$$= \frac{3.83N1+3.90N2+4.20N3+4.21N4}{N1+N2+N3+N4}$$

$$= \frac{3.83\times50+3.90\times50+4.20\times50+4.21\times50}{200}$$

$$= \frac{191.50+195.00+210.00+210.50}{200}$$

$$= \frac{807}{200}$$

$$= 4.035$$

The analysis of above table indicates that the PNB provides the highest satisfaction to its customers as the combined mean score of different variables which determine the satisfaction of customers on the basis of banking services which is determined by the combined mean which is 4.18. The mean score of the PNB lies in between satisfied or very satisfied. The views expressed by the customers of the PNB are consistent as the SD is insignificant 0.84. In case of SBI the satisfaction of the customer lies in between satisfied and very satisfied as the mean score if 4.04 and the views expressed by the customers is consistent as the score of SD is insignificant 0.91. In case of private sector banks the satisfaction of the customers of HDFC bank is in between neither satisfied nor dissatisfied and satisfied and the mean score of ICICI Bank is in between neither satisfied nor dissatisfied and dissatisfied as the mean score is 2.93 however the score of SD of the HDFC show some inconsistent views of the customers, SD is 1.07 for the HDFC bank. ATM cards and mobile banking service are the highly contributed factors towards the satisfaction of customers in SBI and PNB. Net banking and mobile banking services are the highly contributed factors towards the satisfaction of the customers of ICICI and HDFC banks.

The basic objective of using CAMEL is to analyze performance of selected banks.

In the present study researcher has selected four banks two public sector bank, two private sector banks. Four banks, namely SBI, PNB, ICICI Bank and HDFC Bank.

Sources of Data

CAMEL study is mainly based on secondary data. The relevant data, in this regard is collected from PROCESS Data base of CMIE (Center for Monitoring Indian Economy).

Tool and Techniques of Analysis and Period of Study

For the purpose of research, researcher has used a CAMEL technique for E-Banking analysis of selected banks. The period of study for financial analysis in present study is taken 5 years from 2008-09 to 2013-14. Researcher has used simple statistical measures like mean and standard deviation. For testing hypothesis researcher has used F-test

What is CAMEL?

Camel is a technique of ratio analysis which covers five category ratio of banks.

CAMEL stands for

C = Capital Adequacy

A = Asset Quality

M = Management

E = Earning Quality

L = Liquidity

Results and Analysis

Capital Adequacy Ratio

ICICI, HDFC, PNB and SBI banks have maintained the average Capital Adequacy Ratio. All the banks have maintained higher CAR than the prescribed level. According to the norms of RBI, each bank in India has to maintain 8% of their risk-weighted assets as capital with effect from March (2010). However, the growth of CAR is negative in case of all of these banks. The above also holds good with respect to Debt/Equity Ratio. This indicates that the dependence on debt capital has decreased over the last five years in case of all these banks. The ratio of advances of assets is found higher in case of SBI than ICICI, HDFC and PNB banks. The same is also confirmed by F-test which indicates a significant difference in this ratios of the all the banks under reference. The HDFC, and SBI have outperformed ICICI in terms of the growth rate in this ratio (the percentage of advances to total assets). As regards the ratio of government securities to total investments. The difference between all four banks on this count is found significant, which indicates the supremacy of SBI and PNB over ICICI and HDFC in terms of the ratio of Government Securities to Total Investments. Interestingly, this ratio indicates an increasing trend of all banks. Hence the approach of all the banks is turning as conservative.

Assets Quality

The assets quality ratios have registered a declining trend over the years. In so far as the absolute values of the above mentioned asset quality ratios are concerned, no significant difference between ICICI, HDFC and SBI is revealed.

The researcher observed that almost each ratio indicates uptrend irrespective of the bank concerned. The ratio of Total Advances to Total Deposits is an indicator of the management's efficiency in converting the deposits into high earning advances. Hence, the ICICI bank has turned more efficient than the HDFC and SBI in so far as the speed of converting deposits into advances is concerned. The ratios of Business per Employee and Profit per Employee are found higher in case of ICICI, wherein the means of these two ratios found at a very level in case of all the banks.

Earnings Quality

The position of ICICI, HDFC and SBI banks that has emerged on the basis of various ratios used as indicator of earning quality of a bank as per the CAMEL model.

While SBI has outperformed ICICI and HDFC in terms of interest income to total income, the opposite is true in regard to the ratio of noninterest income to total income. The significance of this difference is confirmed by the results of F- test in respect to the ratio of spread to total assets, interest income to total income and non-interest income to total income.

Liquidity

Table below depicts the liquidity position of ICICI, HDFC, and SBI banks. It is shows that all banks indicate upward trend in Liquid Assets to Total Assets Ratio.

The liquidity position of SBI and PNB are sounder as compared to ICICI and HDFC. In case of Government Securities to Total Assets, HDFC is sounder than ICICI and SBI. ICICI bank has outperformed HDFC and SBI in so far as the ratio of Liquid Assets to Demand Deposits and Liquid Assets to Total Deposits are concerned. An attempt is also made to determine whether the liquidity ratios of ICICI, HDFC, PNB and SBI bank differ significantly. The result indicates significant difference between the liquidity positions of all the banks only in terms of one liquidity ratio (i.e. G-Secs to Total Assets) out of ratios. Hence, there is no acknowledgeable difference in the liquidity position of the four banks under reference.

Overall Ranking: As stated in the initial part of this research study, CAMEL Model is used for rating banks according to their performance. Here, we have made an attempt to rank the two sector banks under consideration.

Observation

The researcher makes an attempt to examine and compare the performance of the four banks of India - ICICI a Private Sector Bank, HDFC a Private Sector Bank, PNB a Public Sector Bank and SBI a Public Sector Bank. The analysis is based on CAMEL Model. The study has bought out many interesting results, some of which are mentioned as follows:

- All four banks have succeeded in maintaining CAR at a higher level than the RBI norms.
- The dependence on debt capital has decreased over the last three years in case of all three banks.
- The Asset Quality Ratios (Gross NPA to Net Advances, Net NPA to Net Advances and Net NPAs to Total Assets) have registered increasing trend in ICICI bank, while in HDFC and in SBI it registered fluctuating trends. Thus, it indicates need to take step to reduce in NPA for improvement in the asset quality position of all four banks.
- The investment policy of SBI and PNB is conservative in comparison to ICICI and HDFC.
- Management efficiency of ICICI is better than other selected banks, because business per employee and profit per employee is higher.
- The earning quality, measured in terms of the ratio of Operating Profit to Average Working Fund, Net Profit to Average Assets etc., shows that ICICI bank has outperformed to other selected banks.
- The liquidity ratios (i.e., Liquid Assets to Total Assets and G-Secs to Total Assets) indicates better liquidity positions of all the banks. However SBI has an edge, over ICICI, if compared with each other according to these ratios.

Concept

Banking has never been more important to our society than it is today. Advancement in communication and computer technology and the availability of the internet have made it possible that one can do most banking transactions from remote locations. Information technology is becoming an important factor in the development of financial services sector, especially in banking. E-banking has been viewed as an advanced upgrading from previous electronic delivery systems to open many new business **vistas for the banking sector.** Due to globalisation and entry of new players in the market, the financial sector, particularly the banking sector needs to develop solutions to build a clear and distinct identity. Internet has changed the operations of many businesses, and has become a powerful channel for business marketing and communication. The banking industry has followed this trend in recent years. Information technology has an enormous effect in developing more flexible and user-friendly banking services. Today, e-banking has received greater attention in the banking area; moreover the clients are adopting internet based banking services. In view of all this, the banking system has been attempting to gather more and more information: on aspects that encourage people to do their banking over the internet. In order to reap the benefits of having loyal customers and gaining a competitive advantage online, banks need to develop an understanding of the antecedents of loyalty on the World Wide Web (e-loyalty), such as business factors or personal characteristic. To develop e-loyalty among consumers, bankers must explore influencing variables. This holds especially true for those industries which already depend heavily on their reputation and long-lasting relationships in the offline world, as in the case with the banking sector. The widespread adoption of e-banking services calls for research investigating those factors which are responsible for keeping customers motivated.

The two-fold objective of this work is to study the impact of demographic factors on the use of e-banking services and to explore the motivational factors encouraging the users towards e-banking. The research attempts to test the following hypotheses:

H1 : There is no impact of age on various motivational factors for use of e-banking services.

H2 : There is no impact of income on various motivational factors for use of e-banking services.

H3 : There is no impact of occupation on various motivational factors for use of e-banking services.

H4 : There is no impact of education on various motivational factors for use of e-banking services.

As the concept of e-banking in the emerging scenario is quite new, the present study is both exploratory and descriptive in nature. Accordingly, the data are collected using both primary as well as secondary sources through convenience sampling.

Primary data are collected by administering a pre-tested structured questionnaire to 300 e-banking users residing in Chandigarh, Jaipur and Abohar. The secondary information has been obtained from the reports of RBI, different banks, websites, magazines, journals and newspapers. The collected data are analyzed with the help of percentages, averages, standard deviations and ANOVA to arrive at concise and concrete results.

Analysis and Interpretation

This section presents the respondents' classification according to demographic variables and offers interpretation of the motivational factors with respect to each of them. The profile of the respondents as depicted in below Table shows that majority of them (54.3 percent) belong to the age group of 21 to 35 years, have an income of up to Rs 4 lakhs p.a. (46.0 percent) and are mostly in service class (37.9 percent) with an education level of post graduation and above (67.8 percent).

Table: 5 Demographic Characteristics of sampled respondents

	Demographics	No. of Respondents	Percentage
Age	21-35 yrs.	129	33.7
	36-50 yrs.	208	54.3
	51 yrs. and above	46	12.0
Income	Less than Rs 2 lakhs p.a.	95	24.8
	Rs 2 to Rs 4 lakhs p.a.	176	46.0
	Above Rs 4 lakhs p.a.	112	29.2

(Contd...)

Occupation	Business	101	26.4
	Service	145	37.9
	Professionals	122	31.9
	Others	15	3.8
Education	Matric and under graduate	14	3.7
	Graduate but under postgraduate	109	28.5
	Postgraduate and above	260	67.8

The study sought to assess the importance of motivational factors encouraging customers for e-banking usage. The respondents were provided with six different statements pertaining to motivational factors and their views on them were sought as to how far they motivated them (Table 2). The results revealed that out of six factors, 'time saving' was considered as a very important motivational factor, followed by 'convenient accessibility'; 'accurate information', 'efficient services', 'cost effectiveness' and 'security provision'. It signifies that banks in India lack in providing sufficient security.

A significant percentage (77.1%, taking 'strongly agree' and 'agree' statements together) agreed that 'cost effectiveness' feature of e-banking motivates them for its usage. Very large percentage of the respondents (AS 98.4 %) in the study felt that e-banking is 'conveniently accessible'. Quite importantly, 89 percent of users held that e-banking provides 'accurate information'. Similarly, 89 percent of them believed that 'provision of efficient services' is also one of the motivational factors. Almost 65 percent of respondents agreed that doing banking through e-banking is 'secure'. A large percentage (93.7%) of respondents said that e-banking transactions save time.

In order to get a better understanding of the motivational features encouraging respondents for e-banking usage, the impact of demographic factors like age, income, occupation and education of the sampled respondents were analyzed through ANOVA (Table 3).

Age

Some significant differences were found among the age groups of sampled respondents in terms of their perception of motivational factors. As far as the 'cost effectiveness' of e-banking is concerned, it is perceived differently across different age groups. Young users falling in the age group of 21-35 years agreed (mean score-1.86) whereas middle age users of 36-50 years (mean score 2.17) and old age users of 51 and above years (mean score 2.20) agreed only to some extent that cost effectiveness of e-banking motivates them. The reason for such differences may be the fact that young users are very energetic and assign greater importance to economy of time. They perceive that time saved due to e-banking can be invested in some other fruitful activities.

Similarly, 'accuracy of information' of e-banking is perceived differently by young, middle and old age users. Young users believed more strongly (mean score 1.63) than the middle age (mean score 1.81) and old age users (mean score 1.91) that correctness of information motivates them towards e-banking usage.

While responding to the statement- 'efficient services'-there was a significant difference between the perception of the young age users (mean score 1.46), middle age (mean score 1.76) and old age users (mean score 1.84). One can argue that the young users get more fascinated by proficient services of e-banking than other users. Statistically, the hypothesis gets accepted from the standpoint of 'time saving', 'convenient accessibility' and 'security provision'. However, it gets rejected with regard to other factors, including 'cost effectiveness', 'accurate information' and 'efficient services'. On the whole, it may be concluded that age structure has a significant impact on motivational factors for using the e-banking services. (HI).

Income

While assessing the motivational factors income groups seemed to play a significant role. Respondents falling in the income group of less than Rs 2 lakhs p.a. (mean score 1.83) agreed more than the users having income of Rs 2 to 4 lakhs p.a. (mean score 2.26) and Rs 4 lakhs and above p.a. (mean score 2.29) on the issue of 'cost effectiveness' of e-banking. One can argue that the people having less income are more concerned with the cost of services; consequently this feature of e-banking motivates them.

As far as 'convenient accessibility' is concerned, marked differences were found among the users in various income groups. Respondents in the income group of above Rs 4 lakhs p.a. (mean score 1.17) agreed more than the respondents in the income group of less than Rs 2 lakhs p.a. (mean score 1.23) and Rs 2 to 4 lakhs p.a. (mean score 1.45) regarding convenient accessibility as a motivational factor. The reason for such differences could be the fact that people with high income generally have voluminous and frequent transactions with the bank so they want e-banking services near their places for ease in transactions.

Regarding 'accuracy of information' of e-banking services, there was difference among different income groups. Respondents falling in the lowest income group (mean score 1.60) are more motivated by accuracy than the users in the income group of Rs 2 to 4 lakhs p.a. (mean score 1.80) and Rs 4 lakhs and above p.a. (mean score 1.83). Precisely, there is inverse relationship between income level and need for precise information. That is, lower the income level, higher is the interest expressed in precise information. Statistically, the hypothesis stands accepted with respect to 'time saving', 'efficiency of services' and 'security provision', whereas it is rejected with regard to the remaining factors like 'cost effectiveness', 'accurate information' and 'convenient accessibility'. To conclude, the income level has a significant impact on motivational factors for the use of e-banking services.

Occupation

The ANOVA result revealed that respondents of service class (mean score 1.87) and business class (mean score 1.92) agreed more that 'cost effectiveness' of e-banking motivates them than the professionals (mean score 2.39) and other respondents (mean score 2.40).

Similarly, 'accuracy of information' as a motivating factor is perceived differently among service class (mean score 1.71), business class (mean score 1.72), professionals (mean score 1.79) and others (mean score 2.27). Respondents in service, business and professions agreed more strongly than other respondents that correctness of information encouraged them to use e-banking. Statistically, the hypothesis gets accepted in case of 'convenient accessibility', 'efficient services', 'security provision' and 'time saving', whereas it is rejected in case of 'cost effectiveness' and 'accuracy of information.' It is thus clear from the findings that occupations bear a relationship with the motivational factors (H3). Our findings are in line with those of Stavins (2001) who identified that white-collar consumers are most likely to use e-banking. It can be postulated that occupation status is positively related to the choice of e-banking.

Table 6 : Significant Demographics vis-à-vis Motivational Factors (Summarised output of Analysis of Variance)

Motivational Factors	Demographics	Mean	SD	F-Test	Sig.
Cost affective	21-35	1.86	0.92	3.53	0.03
	36-50	2.17		1.15	
	51 and above	2.20	1.33		
Age Accuracy of (In year) Information	21-35	1.63	0.64	3.80	0.02
	36-50	1.81	0.67		
	51 and above	1.91	1.01		
Efficient services	21-35	1.46	0.50	4.89	0.01
	36-50	1.76	0.73		
	51 and above	1.84	0.80		
Cost affective	Less than Rs 2 lakhs p.a.	1.83	0.82	7.96	0.00
	Rs 2 lakhs to Rs 4 lakhs p a.	2.26		1.32	
	Above Rs 4 lakhs p.a.	2.29	1.23		
Convenient Income accessibility	Less than Rs 2 lakhs p.a.	1.23	0.42	7.61	0.00
	Rs 2 lakhs to Rs 4 Lakhs p.a.	1.45	0.81		
	Above Rs 4 lakhs p.a.	1.17	0.38		
Accurate Information	Less than Rs 2 lakhs p.a.	1.60	0.75	3.27	0.04
	Rs 2 lakhs to Rs 4 lakhs p.a.	1.80	0.80		
	Above Rs 4 lakhs p.a.	1.83	0.48		
Cost effective	Business	1.92	1.01	6.34	0.00
	Service	1.87	0.94		
	Professionals	2.39	1.28		
Occupations Accurate Information	Others	2.40	1.24		
	Business	1.72	071	2.96	0.03
	Service	1.71	0.72		
	Professionals	1.79	0.71		
	Others	2.27	0.59		
Accurate Information Education	Matric and under Graduate	1.71	0.47	8.35	0.00
	Graduate but under	1.99	0.83		
	Postgraduate	1.71			
	Postgraduate and above	1.67		0.65	

Education

In the ANOVA results, it is revealed that education of the respondents also has an impact on the motivational factors in use of e-banking. As far as 'accuracy of information' is concerned, it is perceived differently across different education levels. Users, who were post-graduates and above (mean score 1.67) and graduates but under post-graduate (mean score 1.71) agreed more as compared to the users who were matric and under graduate (mean score 1.99) that accuracy of information motivates them for using e-banking.

Statistically, the hypothesis is accepted, in case of 'cost effectiveness', 'convenient accessibility', 'efficient services', 'security provision' and 'time saving'. On the other hand, it stands rejected with regard to 'accuracy of information'. So, it may be concluded that there is significant impact of motivational factors on the use of e-banking services on the basis of education (H4). These findings are inline with Stavins' (2001) study which showed that as the educational level of consumers increases, their adoption of e-banking would increase as well.

Conclusion

The banking sector in India is undergoing major changes due to competition and the advent of technology. The customer is looking for quality services which can provide him/her satisfaction. This study reveals the customers satisfaction level of public and private sector banks and their comparison. The analysis of data brings out the following conclusions:

- It is evident that State Bank of India has been more sincere in solving and handling of customers' complaints in the present study.
- It is found that the employees of the SBI have been maximum courtesy with their customers, more willing to help customers, more knowledgeable in answering customers' questions, and excellent in giving information to their customers.

- In public sector banks namely SBI and PNB, the knowledge of the banks staff, helpfulness nature of bank staff and courtesy of the bank staff are highly contributed factors towards satisfaction of the customers.
- In private sector banks, knowledge of staff is the highly contributed factor towards satisfaction of the customers of the ICICI Bank and courtesy of the staff and quality of information received is the highly contributed factor towards satisfaction of the customers of the HDFC Bank.
- These findings propose that the employees of public sector banks are very attentive towards its customers as compared to private sector banks.
- ATM cards and cheque book service are the highly contributed factors towards the satisfaction of customers in public sector banks namely the SBI and the PNB.
- In private sector banks, Net-Banking and cheque book services are the highly contributed factors towards satisfaction of the customers of the ICICI and the HDFC Banks.
- It is evident that public sector banks provide excellent services to its customers as compared to private sector banks.
- It was found that proper reception at the counter and improvement in speed of cheque deposits is badly needed by the Punjab National Bank, which will greatly enhance.
- The findings of the study purpose that customers of public sector banks are more satisfied with their accounts and deposits of the banks than private sector banks.

It can be concluded that public sector banks provides better services to their customers than the private sector banks. The customers of public sector banks are more satisfied with traditional banking services such as (ATM; Demand Draft and Cheque Book Facilities) and Bank Accounts as compared to private sector banks whereas customers of private sector banks are more satisfied with counter services such as cash deposit, cash payment, issue a draft, cheque payment and cheque deposit provided by the bank.

Analysis and Interpretation

When planning to initiate a new idea, like e-banking, bankers would like to predict whether it will be acceptable to the users and diagnose the reason why a planned system is not fully acceptable and to take corrective action to find out the factors which motivate the users. It is found that 'time saving' is the most encouraging factor. On the other hand, people are not happy with the security measures. The results of the study also indicate that there is significant impact of demographics on the use of e-banking services. It is observed that age, income, occupation and educational levels of respondents influence the motivational factors. No significant differences were found among respondents regarding 'time saving' and 'security provision' feature of e-banking.

A managerial implication of the findings of this research study is that banks must be aware of the problems of their customer base using e-banking services. Banks should ensure proper security measures without any extra charge for them. This is urgently required in order to face the cut throat competition. In addition to extending our understanding of consumer behaviour in e-banking context, the analysis presents practical implications for policymakers who have to make strategies and take decisions in order to cater to the needs of their consumers.

Financial sector reforms and deregulation of banking sector in 1991 led to the emergence of new generation private sector banks and foreign banks with better technology and products. Consequently, the competition in banking has increased immensely and particularly at metro and urban centers. Delivering quality service to customers is a must for success and survival in today's competitive banking environment. Provision of high quality services enhances Customer's retention rates and helps attract new customers. The significant and positive service qualities of banks, influencing customer, satisfaction are Responsiveness, Tangibles and Empathy. The customers' perception about various dimensions of service quality is not up to, their level of expectation in all three groups of banks. Nationalised banks are lagging behind in all service quality factors compared with their counterparts of private banks. This requires a drastic change in outlook and the way in which the nationalised banks are functioning in this high volatile and competitive environment.

Delivering quality service to customers is a must for success and survival in today's competitive banking environment (Samli and Fronhlich, 1992). Provision of high quality services enhances customers retention rates, helps attract new customers through word of mouth advertising, increases productivity, leads to higher market shares, lowers staff turnover and operating costs, and improves employees' morale, financial performance and profitability (Julian and Ramaseshan, 1994; Lewis, 1993). Financial institutions are acknowledging the customer needs in designing and delivering services, as technical superiority will bring success (Zeithaml and Bitner, 1996). New marketing concepts and strategies (Ennew *et al.*, 1993) focus more on identifying Customer needs and expectation (Morgan, 1989) which prompt them to offer high quality service (Lewis, 1993; Thwaites and Vere, 1995).

Service quality must be guided by what customers want (BMA, 1991) which is embodied in customer perception. Deviance from perceived service quality is defined as the extent of discrepancy between expectation and perception about actual performance (Zeithaml *et al.*, 1990). Consequently, effective management of the determinants of expectation of quality and perception is required (Berry *et al.*, 1985). Although Zeithaml and Bitner (1996); Sharma and Mehta (2005) and Peter *et al.*, (1997) suggest that, as customers might hold similar levels for a spectrum of service firms in the same industry; it would be of interest to explore if service expectations are the same for different groups of banks.

Before the financial sector reforms, the public sector banks in India dominated the banking industry. The primary objective of the public sector banks is to execute the schemes formulated by the Planning Commission of India and the Ministry of Finance, India. They concentrate more on the social welfare and the balanced economic development in India. Financial sector reforms and deregulation of banking sector, 1991 led to the emergence of new generation private sector banks and foreign banks with better technology, lean and nimble footed structure and market oriented products and services and competition in banks has increased immensely, particularly at metro and urban centers. After implementation of Narasimham Committee's recommendations on financial sector reforms, a paradigm shift has been witnessed in the banking sector. This is reflected in profitability. The profit per employee of the Public Sector and Private Sector Banks during 2002-2003 was Rs 1.77 lakh and Rs 4.49 lakh respectively (Swami, 2004) which must have been caused by better Service Quality of the later group of Banks. The technology has helped banks to offer services to more customers and offer narrative products which are tailor made for different needs of individuals.

In India, a number of studies have been conducted to examine the service quality of commercial banks. Sharma and Mehta (2004) revealed that the public sector banks are ahead of private sector banks regarding the customers' perception on the service quality. Verma and Vohra (2000) identified the important factors of service-quality in State Bank of India. Gani and Bhat (2003) identified that the service quality of foreign banks is comparatively better than that of Indian banks. Purohit (2006) found that the service quality provides a valuable tool for measurement of consumer satisfaction. Elango and Gudep (2006) identified that the public sector banks lag behind in all the eight factors of service quality compared with private sector and foreign banks. Rahman (2005) pointed out that the higher service quality gap is noticed in the case of 'reliability' dimension of the commercial banks. Joshua and Koshi (2005) reveal that the service quality of new generation banks is higher than that of the old generation banks. However, there is no specific Study of the impact of service quality on customers' satisfaction in Nationalised Banks, State Bank Groups and Private Sector Banks. Apart from this, an important aspect of distinction between these two groups of banks regarding their customer's perception need to be analysed. Hence, the present study focuses on the fulfillment of this research gap with specific objectives.

- To identify the important factors of service quality in commercial banks;

- To ascertain the perception of customers regarding the service quality of banks;
- To analyse and compare the perception of the customers about Public Sector Banks and Private Sector Banks;
- To examine the impact of perception of service quality on the customers satisfaction; and
- To identify the discriminating factors of service quality among the two group of banks.

Quality has been defined as superiority or excellence (Taylor and Baker, 1994), or, Consumer's overall impression of the relative inferiority/ superiority of the organisation and its services (Bitner and Hulbert, 1994; Keiningham *et al.,* 1995). Customer expectations are beliefs about the service. The quality of service is judged by the best performance which is treated as standard against which the performance is judged (Zeithaml *et al.,* 1993); What customer's think a service provider should offers rather than what is on offer may be defined as service qualify (Parasuraman *et al.,*1988). Expectations are formed on the basis of a variety of sources such as the customers' personal needs and wishes (Edvardsson *et al.,* 1994), the customer's personal philosophy about a particular service, by promises (staffs, advertising and other communications), by implicit service promises (such as price and the tangibles associated with the service), by words of mouth communication (with other customers, friends, family and experts) as well as by past experience of that service (Zeithaml and Bitner, 1996).

Perceived service quality has been defined as the customer's global attitude or judgment of the overall excellence or superiority of the service. It results from comparison by consumers of expectations with their perception of service delivered by the suppliers (Lewis *et al.,* 1994; Taguchi and Quelch, 1983). The four major factors, influencing customer perception of service, are in service encounter (Gronroos, 1990; Bitner *et al.,* 1990); evidence of service (Wong and Perry, 1991); and image and reputation (Keller, 1993); and price (Kangis and Passa, 1997). In service encounter, the verbal and non-verbal behaviour, is an important determinant of quality just like tangible cues such as equipment and physical setting. The evidence of service reveals that the customers are searching for cues to help themselves to determine the level of service. Image and reputation reflect the associations held in the memory of the consumer. The price indicates the customer perception of the price paid for service quality.

Service quality was operationalised by using Parasuraman *et. al.;* it has (1988) widely known 22 parameters. Five of these components are Tangibles, Reliability, Responsiveness, Assurance and Empathy which are SERVQUAL instrument. SERVQUAL is criticized by Bala and Boiler (1992), Cronin and Taylor (1994) and Me Alexander *et al.* (1994). They revealed the importance of SERVPERF scale to measure the service quality. In the Indian context, Elango and Gudep (2006) and Zillur Rahman (2005) used 21 statements to measure the service quality in Public, Private and Foreign Banks. Prabhakaran and Satya (2003) used seven dimensions of banks; namely Service dimension, Service attributes, Reliability/ Responsiveness, Assurance, Empathy and Tangibles to measure the service quality of banks.

Dhar *et al.* (2004) identified thirty nine variables to analyse the service difference in Public and Private Sector Banks. In the present study, 21 statements have been used to measure the service quality in commercial banks. The respondents were asked to rate the 21 statements on a five point scale in two different dimensions, according to their expectation and perception about the service offered by banks (Brown *et al.,* 1993; and Carman; 1990).

Customers' satisfaction was operationalised by a five item measure. These items are related to the five values of SERVQUAL. The items included are the appearance of bank's physical facilities, equipment, personnel and communication material; the ability of the bank to perform the promised service dependably and the willingness of the bank to help customers and provide prompt service; the knowledge and courtesy of the bank's employees and their ability to convey trust and confidence, caring and individualised attention the bank provides to its customers.

To identify the important service quality factors in banking, the scores of 21 service quality variables have been taken into account. The factor analysis has been executed to examine the service quality variables and decompose them into important service quality factors.

Before conducting factor analysis, the validity of data for factor analysis has been examined with the help of KMO measures and Bartlett's test of sphere city.

The computed KMO measures and chi-square value satisfy the validity of data for factor analysis. The KMO measure is greater than 0.5 at zero percent level of significance of Chi-square (Rao and Saikia, 2006). The factor analysis results in five important service quality factors. The factor loadings of the service quality variables, its reliability co-efficient, the Eigen values and the percent of variance explained by the service quality factors are shown in table.

Table 7: Factor Loading of the Variables in Service Quality

Factors Variables in Service		Factor Loading	Reliability Co- efficient	Eigen Value	Per cent of Variation explained
Reliability	Providing service as promised	0.8683	0.7149	3.8541	18.48
	Sincere in Solving the problem	0.8104			
	Performing service right the first time	0.7523			
	Providing service at the promised time	0.7088			
	Maintaining error-free records				
Respon-siveness	Customers informed about service performance	0.9027	0.7944	3.3019	16.07
	Providing prompt service to customers	0.8633			
	Willing to help customers	0.7396			

(Contd...)

	Employee's readiness to customers request	0.7161			
Assurance	Employees are trust worthy	0.8608	0.8936	2.4542	13.14
	Customers feel comfortable interacting with employees	0.7911			
	Employees are knowledgeable	0.6994			
Tangible	Up - to - date equipment	0.8668	0.7331	2.0696	10.45
	Visually appealing facilities	0.8143			
	Neat and professional appearance of employees	0.7346			
	Communication material	0.6961			
	Banks give individual attention	0.9114	0.7091	1.5462	9.66
Empathy	Convenient operating hours	0.7862			
	Employees understand the needs of customers	0.7417			
	Employee has the best interest at heart	0.6069			

The important factors are 'Reliability' and 'Responsiveness'. The 'Reliability' factor consists of five variables and 'Responsiveness' factor consists of four variables. The most important variables in the above two factors are improved service as promised and informed customers about service performance.

The third and fourth factors extracted from the factor analysis, are 'assurance' and 'tangible' factors. The last factor is 'empathy'. The five factors of Reliability, Responsiveness, Assurance, Tangibles and Empathy are included for further analysis on the identification of service quality gap (difference between perception and expectation.

In the Nationalised Banks, the mean expectation on all dimensions in service quality except Reliability, is higher than the mean of perception. In case of 'Reliability', the mean perception among the customers is higher than its expectation. But the difference is not statistically significant. The mean difference between the perception and expectation on Tangibles.

The mean of perception and expectation of five dimensions of service quality among the customers in four groups of banks have been measured to analyse the significant difference between the mean of perception and expectation on each dimension of service quality factors among the customers in two groups of banks. Responsiveness, Assurance and Empathy are statistically significant, since the calculated values of 't' are greater than table value at five percent level of probability. The difference between mean of perception and expectation is higher in the dimensions of service quality factors, namely Assurance and Empathy. Among the customers of Public Sector Bank Group, the mean perception is lesser than the mean expectation regarding all five dimensions of service quality. But the mean differences of service quality reflected by Responsiveness, Assurance and Empathy are statistically significance. The mean perception of reliability is greater than the mean expectation among the customers in private sector banks. But the difference between these two means is not statistically significant. In all other four aspects of service quality, the mean expectation is greater than the mean perception. The significant difference between the mean perception and expectation also exists for 'Empathy'. It reveals that the customers of private Sector Banks do not find their service upto expectation in four factors of quality though these differences are not statistically significant. The significant and higher difference among the mean perception and expectation exists among the customers in Public Sector Banks, followed by customers of Public Sector Bank Groups. It reveals the higher service quality gap in the above said two groups of banks compared to private banks.

The customers of nationalised banks, Public Sector Bank group and the private sector banks have been analyzed. The perception of various dimensions of service quality among three groups of customers may differ from one another. It is highly imperative to understand what discriminates service quality among the three groups of customers for policy implications. In order to analyse the significant discriminant dimensions of service quality, multi discriminant analysis has been used. The scores on perception of five different dimensions of service quality are included for estimating of multi discriminant function. The unstandardised procedure has been followed to estimate the function.

The study of bank service quality has identified such service quality factors as Reliability, Responsiveness, Assurance, Tangibles and Empathy. The significantly influencing service quality factors of banks on customers' satisfaction are Responsiveness, Tangibles and Empathy which made a positive impact on customers' satisfaction also.

REFERENCES

1. Mattila, M. Karjaluoto, H. and Fento, T. (2001), "Internet Banking Adoption Factors in Finland", *Journal of Internet Banking and Commerce, Online International Referred Journal,* available at: www.arravdev.com Vol. 6, No. 1.
2. Mattila, M., Kaijaluoto, H. and Fento, T. (2002), "Electronic Banking in Finland: Consumer Beliefs and Reactions to a New Delivery Channel", *Journal of Financial Services Marketing,* Vol. 6, No, 4, pp. 346-361.
3. Mishra, A. K., "Internet Banking in India Part-1", available at: http - www.banknetindia.com/bankina/ibka.htm
4. Nor, K., Pearson, M. J. (2007), "The Influence of Trust on Internet Banking Acceptance", *Journal of Internet Banking and Commerce, Online International Referred Journal*, available at: www.arraudeu.coin Vol. 12, No. 2.
5. Padachl, K., Rojid, S., Seetanah, B. (2008), Investigating into the factors that influence the adoption of internet banking in Mauritius", *Journal of Internet Business,* Issue 5, 99-120.
6. Pikkarainen, T., Karjaluoto, Hi and Pahnila, S. (2004), "Consumer acceptance of online banking; an extension of the technology acceptance model", *Internet Research,* Vol. 14, No. 3, pp. 224-235.
7. Singh and Malhotra (2004), "Status of Internet Bonking in India", *Management Accountant,* Vol. 39, No. II, pp. 890-896.
8. Singhal, D. and Padmanabhan, V. (2008), "A Study on Customer Perception Towards Internet Banking: Identifying Major Contributing Factors", *The Journal of Nepalese Business Studies,* Vol. 5, No. I, pp. idi-iii.

9. Stavins, J. (2001), "Effect of Consumer Characteristics on the Use of ftiyment Instruments", *New England Economic Review,* No. 3, pp. 19- 3i.

10. Sulaiman, A., Lim, C.H., and Wee, A. (2005), "Prospects and Challenges/ of E-Banking in Malaysia", *Electronic Journal on Information Systems in Developing Countries,* Vol. 22, No.l, pp. 1-11.

11. Peterson, R.A. (1994), "A meta analysis of cronbachs coefficient alpha", *Journal of Consumer Research*; September, pp. 381-391.

12. Prabhakaran, S. and Satya, S. (2003), "An insight into service attributes in banking sector", *Journal of Service Research*, 3(1), April- September, pp. 157-169.

13. Prasada, Rao, and Vendantam Saikia (2006), "Mutual funds: Exploring the Retail Customer Expectation", *The ICFAI Journal of Services Marketing*, 4(2); pp. 25-33.

14. Shainesh, G. and Sharma, Tanuja (2003), "Linkages between service climate and service quality- A study of banks in India, IIMB", Management Review, 5(3) September, pp. 74-81.

15. Sharma, Alka and Mehta, Versha (2005), "Service quality perception in Journal Services-A case study of banking services". *Journal of Services Research,* 4(2), October 2004 - March 2005, pp. 205-221.

16. Sheetal, B. Sachdev and Harsh V. Verma (2002) "Customer expectations and service quality dimension consistency," *Journal of Management Research,* 2(1) pp. 43-52.

17. Swami, B.K. (2004). "Indian Banks in 2010: Emerging Scenario", *IBA Bulletin,* 26(1), January, pp. 161-164.

18. Verma, D.P.S. and Vohra, Ruchika (2000), "Customer Perception of Banking service quality: A Study of State Bank of India", *The Journal of Institute of Public Enterprise,* 23(3&4), pp. 46-54.

- **Credit card customers:** Credit card users have a lot in store. With Internet banking, customers can not only pay their credit card bills online but also get a loan on their cards. Not just this, they can also apply for an additional card, request a credit line increase and God forbid if you lose your credit card, you can report lost card online.
- **Railway pass:** Indian Railways has tied up with ICICI bank and you can now make your railway pass for local trains online. The pass will be delivered to you at your doorstep. But the facility is limited to Mumbai, Thane, Nasik, Surat and Pune. The bank would just charge Rs 10 + 12.24 percent of service tax.
- **Investing through Internet banking:** Opening a fixed deposit account cannot get easier than this. An FD can be opened online through funds transfer. Online banking can also be a great friend for lazy investors. Now investors with interlinked demat account and bank account can easily trade in the stock market and the amount will be automatically debited from their respective bank accounts and the shares will be credited in their demat account.

  Moreover, some banks even give the facility to purchase mutual funds directly from the online banking system. So it removes the worry about filling those big forms for mutual funds, they will now be just a few clicks away. Nowadays, most leading banks offer both online banking and demat account. However if the customer have there demat account with independent share brokers, then need to sign a special form, which will link your two accounts.
- **Recharging your prepaid phone:** Now there is no need to rush to the vendor to recharge the prepaid phone, every time the talk time runs out. Just top-up the prepaid mobile cards by logging in to Internet banking. By just selecting the operator's name, entering the mobile number and the amount for recharge, the phone is again back in action within few minutes.
- **Shopping at your fingertips:** Leading banks have tie ups with various shopping websites. With a range of all kind of

products, one can shop online and the payment is also made conveniently through the account. One can also buy railway and air tickets through Internet banking.

E-Banking refers to performing basic banking transactions by customers round the clock globally through Electronic Media. In other words, E-Banking is the application of IT infrastructure with latest equipment and solutions and integrated networks essentially to facilitate smooth and efficient payment and settlement, improved customer service and the resultant increase in profitability aspects of e-banking includes Easy Access to Customers, Inter-bank Transactions, Electronic Central Banking, Intranet Procurement.

The popularity which virtual banking services have won among customers, owing to the speed, convenience and round-the-clock access they offer, is likely to increase in the future. However, several issues of concern would need to be pro-actively attended. While most of electronic banking have built-in security features such as encryption, prescriptions of maximum monetary limits and authorisations, the system operators have to be extremely vigilant and provide clear-cut guidelines for operations. On the larger issue of electronically initiated funds transfer, issues like authentication of payments instructions, the responsibility of the customer for secrecy of the security procedure would also need to be addressed. Main Instruments or Facilities Provided by E-Banking/Innovative Banking Computerisation, ATM Facility, All Day Banking, Anywhere Banking, Net Banking or 'On Line Banking', Mobile Banking or M-Banking, Wireless Application Protocol (WAP), Credit Cards.

Online banking, which can be defined as the provision of information or services by a bank to its customers over the Internet [Daniel, 1999], has been one of the major developments in the financial service sector in recent years. According to a survey conducted by Pew Internet and America Life, online banking has been the fastest growing Internet activity in the US over the last five years. As of November 2004, a total of 53 million Americans (44% of all US Internet users) use some form of online banking service [McGann, 2005]. In Germany the number of online accounts has increased almost tenfold between 1999 and 2004, with 40% of all accounts now being online [Association of German Banks, 2004]. With the number of online banking consumers steadily increasing, the focus of attention shifts from enticing customers to the online world to retaining them. While the focus of the aforementioned papers lies on offline versus online, this paper deals with the problem of how to keep a customer online and loyal to a specific supplier. Therefore, we analyze which antecedents might induce customers to stay with a particular online bank instead of switching suppliers. We will start discussing our model by referring to the concept of loyalty, which has been investigated extensively in the offline world.

From the review of literature, we found that education is one of the crucial factors for expanding e-banking. Younger consumers and males are more comfortable in using e-banking. Convenience and accuracy, feedback and complaint management, efficiency, queue management, accessibility and customisation were found to be primary dimensions of e-banking service quality. However, most of the studies are carried out in foreign countries. In light of the above findings, the present study is undertaken in Indian context to find out bankers perspectives on e-banking and comparative study of selected Public and Private Sector Banks.

Banks have transformed themselves and are offering services through internet. E-banking is defined as the automated delivery of new and traditional banking products and services directly to customers through electronic, interactive communication channels. E-banking includes the systems that enable financial institution customers, individuals or businesses, to access accounts, transact business, or obtain information on financial products and services through a public or private network, including the Internet. Nowadays commercial banks more concentrate on the E-banking services and there is competition in between them. The customer of commercial banks also attract towards e-banking services hence the research study is titled as "A Critical Study of Trends in E-Banking with Special References to Selected Public and Private Sector Banks."

- E-Banking INITIATIVES of PNB includes Under PNB Krishak Saathi (Debt Swap Scheme), the Bank has financed Rs 139.75 crore to 34,459 farmers upto Dec, 2009 for repaying the debt taken from private money lenders, During the 9 months of 2009-10, the Bank conducted 4894 Kisan Gosthies wherein 1.97 lakh farmers benefitted through marketing dissemination of useful information, Bank has operationalised 8 Farmers' Training Centres where more than 46,000 persons have been trained during Apr-Dec, 2009 at Bank's cost including around 9500 women. Around 15,000 animals have been treated at the Animal check-up camps organised by the Bank and around 6000 persons have been provided free medical advice, PNB is the first nationalised bank to implement an Enterprise-wide Data warehouse to integrate Data from multiple source systems and provides MIS and data feed to Anti Money Laundering and Operational Risk Solution. Operational Risk Solution has been operationalised to monitor compliance with BASEL II requirements. ECS (Electronic Clearing System) facility has been provided in 981 branches of the Bank at 49 Centres, Of the 6 PNB Sponsored RRBs, 3 RRBs branches have become 100% CBS. Out of 1389 branches in, 719 branches have been migrated to CBS, Impressive response to bank's 'CASA Campaign' during August-Dec, 2009, more than 16 lakh CASA accounts were opened, to facilitate factoring, forfeiting and trade finance related business, a joint venture company namely M/s India Factoring and Finance Solutions Pvt. Ltd. has been incorporated in Dec '09 in collaboration with FIM Bank (Malta), Banca IFIS (Italy) and Blend Financial Service with our stake being 30%. The Festival Bonanza continues for housing and Car loans till Jan 31, 2010 with rebate in interest rates and processing fees.

- E - Banking Concept of SBI is the nationalised banks are expected to perform much more than merely mobilising the community's savings for purpose of lending to a few selected sectors. Under New Banking Policy loans are purpose worthy instead of security worthy. The purpose of the loan sanctioned is to be of prime importance. Under the old policy adequate security would have justified a loan even for a project of doubtful viability. Traditionally, a banker hardly bothered about the financial analysis and need of the borrower once he is certain about the safety and security offered for the loan. But now a banker advances only when he is satisfied about the genuineness of the financial need of the party. The assessment of genuineness is only possible after analyzing the party's past and projected balance sheet and financial records on objective basis. Hence subjectivity basis changed into objectivity base in the event of advances to borrowers. After nationalisation, the banks have to act as agents of growth in various areas. Under lead bank scheme various banks are surveying the socio-economic resources of the areas allotted to them i.e. not only they collect deposits and advance it to the borrowers but also identify the potentiality of the area. On the eve of nationalisation there were regional disparities in the share of various states both in total bank deposits and advances. The post nationalisation banking policies is concerned with removal of disparities in deposit and advances. The new banking policy aims at correcting the past sectoral imbalances of bank credit by diverting on increasingly large share of new advances towards the priority sectors i.e. agriculture, small scale industries, retail trade, exports, small business, self employed people, education etc.

All branches of SBI are computerised but on decentralised systems, there the initiative of core banking took place in 2008-more than 6500 branches (95% of business) on Core Banking Solution (CBS). Internet Banking facility for Corporate customers were also launched in early 2008. More Interfaces developed with e-Commerce and other sites through alternate channels like ATM and Online Banking. All Foreign Offices were brought on Centralised Solution. Large network is playing the role of backbone for connectivity across the country. Multiple Service Providers are providing the links – BSNL, MTNL, Reliance, Tata and Reliance which are making the system errorless and provide high speed. State Bank of India is India's largest bank with a branch network of over 11000 branches and 6 associate banks located even in the remotest parts of India. State Bank of India (SBI) offers a wide range of banking products and services to corporate and retail customers. "Online SBI" is the Internet banking portal for State Bank of India. The portal provides anywhere, anytime, online access to accounts for State Bank's Retail and Corporate customers. The application is developed using the latest cutting edge technology and tools. The infrastructure supports unified, secure access to banking services for accounts in over 11,000 branches across India.

- The Housing Development Finance Corporation Limited (HDFC) was amongst the first to receive 'in principle' approval from the Reserve Bank of India (RBI) to set up a bank in the private sector, as part of the RBI's liberalisation of the Indian Banking Industry in 1994. The bank was incorporated in August 1994 in the name of 'HDFC Bank Limited', with its registered office in Mumbai, India. HDFC Bank commenced operations as a Scheduled Commercial Bank in January 1995. HDFC Bank comprises of a dynamic and enthusiastic team determined to accomplish the vision of becoming a World-class Indian bank. HDFC bank's business philosophy is based on our four core values - Customer Focus, Operational Excellence, Product Leadership and People. They believe that the ultimate identity and success of their bank will reside in the exceptional quality of people and their extraordinary efforts. They are committed to hiring, developing, motivating and retaining the best people in the industry.

E-Banking in HDFC has always been market-oriented and dynamic with respect to resource mobilisation as well as its lending programme. This renders it more than capable to meet the new challenges that have emerged. Over the years, HDFC has developed a vast client base of borrowers, depositors, shareholders and agents, and it hopes to capitalise on this loyal and satisfied client base for future growth. Internal systems have been developed to be robust and agile, to take into account changes in the volatile external environment. HDFC has developed a network of institutions through partnerships with some of the best institutions in the world, for providing specialised financial services. Each institution is being line-tuned for a specific market, while offering the entire HDFC customer base the highest standards of quality in product design, facilities and service.

- ICICI Bank Ltd. is India's second largest financial services company headquartered in Mumbai, India. It offers a wide range of banking products and financial services to corporate and retail customers through a variety of delivery channels and through its specialised subsidiaries in the areas of investment banking, life and non-life insurance, venture capital and asset management. The Bank has a network of 2,533 branches and 6,800 ATMs in India, and has a presence in 19 countries, including India. The bank has subsidiaries in the United Kingdom, Russia, and Canada; branches in United States, Singapore, Bahrain, Hong Kong, Sri Lanka, Qatar and Dubai International Finance Centre; and representative offices in United Arab Emirates, China, South Africa, Bangladesh, Thailand, Malaysia and Indonesia. ICICI Bank was established in 1994 by the Industrial Credit and Investment Corporation of India, an Indian financial institution, as a wholly owned subsidiary. The parent company was formed in 1955 as a joint-venture of the World Bank, India's public-sector banks and public-sector insurance companies to provide project financing to Indian industry. The bank was initially known as the Industrial Credit and Investment Corporation of India Bank, before it changed its name to the abbreviated ICICI Bank. The parent company was later merged into ICICI Bank.

  ICICI Bank has been at the forefront when it comes to technology adoption in banking sector in India. Business intelligence has been a long journey for the company with 12 million terabyte of data currently. And the reason why ICICI Bank is spending so much on technology is primarily because of two reasons - customer expectations and behaviour is changing rapidly in India and second, the diversified customer base in India.

Conclusion

As the concept of e-banking in the emerging scenario is quite new, the present study is both exploratory and descriptive in nature. Accordingly, the data are collected using both primary as well as secondary sources through convenience sampling. Primary data are collected by administering a pre-tested structured questionnaire to 300 e-banking users residing in Chandigarh, Abohar and Jaipur. The secondary information has been obtained from the reports of RBI, different banks, websites, magazines, journals and newspapers. The collected data are analyzed with the help of percentages, averages, standard deviations and ANOVA to arrive at concise and concrete results.

There is need for strengthening customer service. Investing heavily on advertisement and promotion of new products to attract new customers would prove to be futile, if those customers are subsequently have to leave because of poor customer service. Most banks have not been able to take full advantage of 'cross-selling' of products and services, which is the very essence of E- banking. It is imperative that banks intending to enter/expand E-banking should first identify the segments that they are capable of servicing and accordingly evolve products and services.

With increasing competition among the banks in terms of internet business, the banks need to adopt the desirable strategies such as identifying segments, developing products, developing/using appropriate delivery channels, marketing, management of risk, customer service and retention. Banks while evolving strategies to enter/expand there internet portfolio should not only appreciate the complexities of E-banking but also learn from their past experiences. Designing of clear-cut and comprehensive corporate policy covering strengths and limitations with regard to E-banking is the immediate need of Banks. Banks must build awareness amongst staff in E-banking centers.

Proper assessment of ever-increasing customers' expectations is very important. Innovate and respond to the changing needs of customers in terms of new products and services needs to be looked into. Hence identification of internet segments, maintaining range of products and services for diverse needs of customers, strengthening bank's staff competence in handling products and services is must. Optimal utilisation of the available technology is the need of the hour. Banks need to utilise existing data-base and building ability to 'cross-sell' to increase fee based income of the bank. Apart from this the technology can also be used to build marketing thrust and capturing 'walk-in businesses' effectively. With similar products offered by the banks, service is the only differentiator which makes the difference. In such scenario, service quality and Customer Relationship Management needs special attention to create moment-of-truth for the customer. This will enable the banks to enhance the customer loyalty towards them. The banks should adorn the image of 'most customer friendly' bank by simplifying the banking for them.

Though there are multiple e-delivery channels in the banks, yet the branch banking is important since it creates the personal touch with the customers. However, with the changing demands of the customers, the branches should be transformed from the traditional branches to sales-touch point. The branch personnel should focus on marketing and cross-selling activities and routine task such as account opening/loan processing can be done at the back office level/ centralised hubs. There is Need for 'systematic approach' which is a pre-condition for successful E-banking. In today's life 'Innovation is necessity, not option'. Hence the banks must continue to innovate in terms of products and services to cater to the needs of the vast segment of the society. To innovate, understanding the changing customer/ market needs is fundamental. Banks must function efficiently as service providers. E-banking is moving from class banking to mass banking in a competitive scenario. Customer satisfaction requires innovations to facilitate banking. Banks are moving to rule based lending and facilitating dick banking rather than brick banking.

Promoting E-banking has issues of competition, customer expectations, growing affluence, diversity of products, technology upgradation, demographic trends, collaborations and globalisation in the background of liberalisation. The banks are facing tougher competition, dwindling profit margins and reducing negotiating power. Growing NPA Portfolio has forced the banks to revisit their strategies for E-banking. Focus on customer centricity, product innovation, quick delivery, better customer relationship, formation of marketing teams, leveraging from technology, identification of emerging markets in rural India are the developments that E-banking needs to look into to sustain the profitability of the banks. E-banking has huge growth opportunities in India and it has to conquer many more heights before getting exhausted like its counter parts in developed markets like US and Europe. Hence it is important to understand challenges and bottlenecks faced, along with offering and implementing right solutions.

Banks have started acknowledging the importance of the customers in developing their business. They have recognised that it is essential to protect and grow its customer base and ultimately its profitability. The banks can do this by building a strong relationship with the customers. To meet the customer needs and to beat the competition, they must deliver superior quality service. The MDM approach adopted by banks focuses on maximising the value for the customers and the bank. Finally, the key drivers to customer loyalty are:

- Positive Staff Attitude.
- Honesty, Integrity and Reliability.
- Productive advice and delivery; of the promised service.
- Consistent delivery of superior quality service.
- Simplicity and easiness of doing business.
- A fair and efficient complaints resolution.

Suggestions and Recommendations of the Study

- Public sector banks need to improve their counter services.
- Customers' grievances should be redressed speedily and customers' satisfaction should always be on the top priority.
- Employees should be given training to improve their attitude.
- Banks should arrange meetings with their customers to promptness in providing the services.

- It is advisable for all the banks under study to keep a separate complaint-cum-suggestion box/book to enable customers to offer suggestions and complaints.
- The working hours of the banks must be as flexible as possible. The operating hours of banks must be extended depending upon the needs and desires of customers.
- Provision for separate inquiry counter at all the banks would be very useful especially to the illiterate customers. Efficient, knowledgeable, customers, competent and versatile frontline staff is the prime requirement for all the banks surveyed.
- As so many customers still using ATM cards, so there should be required more ATM machines for the convenience of the customers.
- The banks must try to find put the specific needs of different customers, so that suitable package of services can be made available to them.
- It is believed that the suggestions offered above, if properly implemented, will go a long way in ensuring Customers' Satisfaction in the banks under study.
- Banks should organise Seminar and Conference to educate the customer regarding uses of online banking as well as security and privacy of their account.
- Some customers are hindered by lack of computer skills they need to be educated on basic skills required to conduct online banking.
- Banks must emphasize the convenience that online banking can provide to people such as avoiding long queue in order to motivate them to use it.
- Banks must emphasize the cost saving that online can provide to the people, such as reduce transaction of cost by use of online banking.

Limitations of the Study

The following are the limitations of the study:

- The proposed study will concentrate only on qualitative aspects.

- Random and Stratified sampling technique likely to be applied in the selection of bank customers.
- E-banking promotes lack of socialising/social contacts.
- Hackers may intercept data and defraud customers.
- Phone bills can increase.
- Customers will be more vulnerable to phishing.
- Customers are compelled to have computers at home, Internet access and computer skills.

Contributions to the Study

This study will serve as a beginning of a new movement and breaking new grounds in learning and development of E-Banking in SBI, PNB, HDFC, ICICI Bank. It will serve to promote electronic banking in these banks. With this study, we are committed to move forward.

Further Scope of the Study

My Research basically deals with "**A critical study of trends in E- Banking with special references to selected public and private sector banks".** I have focused on two banks, SBI and PNB in public sector and HDFC and ICICI in private sector and facilities provided in E-Banking by these banks to its valued customers.

I would suggest that further study should deal with the working of foreign banks regarding E-Banking benefits and facilities given by them to its customer. This comparative study would definitely help our banking sector to allure the customers both in private and public sector, thereby contributing to the progress and development of the society and nation. This comparison would bring out the drawbacks in our public sector and private sector E- Banking, and make us aware of the advanced technological developments adopted by foreign banks. So that we can make commendable changes in E- Banking in India both in Private and Public sector.

38. Rakesh Mohan. “Indian banking and e-Security”. Economic developments in India, Vol. 84, 1st Edition, New Delhi: Academic Foundations, 2004.
39. Santhanam – Banking law and practice (2007), Margham Publications.
40. Venugopalan M. “Implementation of core banking solutions to withstand competition” IBA Bulletin, Vol. XXVII, No. 2, February 2005.
41. Vivek Gupta. “Overview”. E-banking –Global perspectives, 1st edition, Hyderabad: ICFAI press, 2002.
42. Zethmi, V.A. Bitner Marijjo and Grenier Dwayene (2008). Services marketing–The McGraw Hill Companies – New Delhi.

Journals and Reports

1. Reserve Bank of India. (1984). Report of the Committee on Mechanisation in Banking Industry.
2. RBI (1989). Report of the committee on computerisation in banks (The Rangarajan committee) Mumbai: Reserve Bank of India.
3. RBI (1998). Report of the committee on Banking sector reforms (The Narsimham committee) Mumbai: Reserve Bank of India.
4. Basel Committee on Banking Supervision (2001). ‘Risk Management Principles for Electronic Banking’, paper 82, May, (www.bis.org).
5. Claessens, S, T Glaessner and Klingebiel (2000). ‘E-finance in Emerging Markets: Is Leapfrogging Possible?’, World Bank Financial Sector Discussion Paper, No. 4, June.
6. Economist (2003). ‘Banking on the Technology Cycle’, The Economist’s Technology Quarterly, September 6, pp. 12-16.
7. Kohli, S S (2003). ‘Indian Banking Sector: Challenges and Opportunities’, Vikalpa, Vol. 28, No. 3, July-September, pp 85-89.
8. Nsouli, S M and A Schaechter (2002). ‘Challenges of the E-banking Revolution’, Finance and Development, International Monetary Fund, September, Volume 39, Number 3.
9. United Nations Conference on Trade and Development (UNCTAD) (2002): E-commerce and Development Report, (http://rO.unctad.org/ ecommerce/ docs/).
10. Mittal, R.K. & Sanjay (2007). “Technology in Banking Sector: Issues and Challenges”, Vinimaya, Vol. XXVII, No. 4, (Jan - March), pp. 14-22.
11. Padhy, K.C. (2007). ‘Banking Future’, (ed.book) Dominant Publishers and Distributors, New Delhi.
12. Shastri, R.V. (2003). “Recent Trends in Banking Industry: IT Emergence”, Analyst, (March).
13. Shetty, V.P. (2000). “E-Banking”, IBA Bulletin, Vol. XXI, No. 3 (March Special Issue), pp. 31-34.

14. Uppal, R.K. & Kaur, R. (2007). "Indian Banking Moving Towards IT", Journal of Commerce and Trade, Vol. 2, No. 1 (April), pp. 26-32.
15. Daniel, E. (1999). Provision of electronic banking in the UK and Republic of Ireland, International Journal of Bank Marketing, Vol. 17(2), pp. 72-82.
16. Durkin, ML, Jennings, D., Mulholland G. and Worthington, S. (2008). I Key influences and inhibitors on adoption of the Internet for banking, Journal of Retailing and Consumer Services, Vol. 15, pp. 348-357.
17. Eriksson, K., Kerem, K., & Nilsson, D. (2008). The adoption of commercial innovations in the former Central and Eastern European markets. The case of internet banking in Estonian, International I Journal of Bank Marketing, Vol. 26 (3), pp. 154-69 Journal of Management and Science, Vol. 2, No. 11, S SN.2249 - 12 60/E I S.
18. Gerrard, P. and Cunningham, J.B. (2003). The Diffusion of internet banking among Singapore consumers, The Journal of Bank Marketing, Vol. 21 (l), pp. 16-28.
19. Gerrard, P., Cunningham, J.B. and Devlin, J.F. (2006). Why consumers are not using internet banking: a qualitative study, Journal of Services Marketing, Vol. 20 (3), pp. 160-168.
20. Grabner-Krauter, S., & Faullant, R. (2008). Consumer acceptance of internet banking: the influence of internet trust, International Journal of Bank Marketing, Vol. 26 (7), pp. 483-504.
21. Guerrero, M. M., Egea, J. M. O. and Gonzalez, M. V. R. (2007). Application of the latent class regression methodology to the analysis of Internet use for banking transactions in the European Union, Journal of Business Research, Vol. 60, pp. 137-145.
22. Hamlet, C. (2000). Community banks go online, American Bankers Association. ABA Journal, Vol. 92(3).
23. Howcroft, B., Hamilton, R. and Heder, P. (2002). Consumer attitude and the usage and adoption of home-based banking in the United Kingdom, International Journal of Bank Marketing, Vol.20 (3), pp. 111-121.
24. Hughes, T. (2001). Market orientation and the response of UK financial services companies to changes in Market conditions as a result e-commerce, International Journal of Bank Marketing, Vol. 19, No. 6, pp. 222-231.
25. Ibrahim, E.E., Joseph, M and Ibeh, K.I.N (2006). Customers perception of electronic service delivery in the UK retail banking sector, International Journal of Bank Marketing, Vol. 24, No. 7, pp. 475-493.
26. Ilett, D., (2005). Online Bankers to Double by 2010, Retrieved on April 2008, http://www.silicon.c0m/financialservices/0,3800010322,395 13014,00.htm.
27. IMRB and IMAI (2006). Internet in India- 2006 (Summary Report of I- Cube, 2006), New Delhi: IMRB International (e-technology Group@IMRB).

28. Kothari, D.(2007). Banks are now just a Click or SMS away, The Week, Vol. 25, No. 48, pp. 63-76.
29. Dos Santos, B.L., Peffers, K.G. and Mauer, D.C. (1993). "The Impact of InformationTechnology Investment Announcements on the Market Value of the Firm", *Information Systems Research*, Vol. 4, pp. 1-23.
30. Brynjolfsson, Erik (1993). "The Productivity Paradox of Information Technology",*Communication of ACM*, Vol. 36(12), pp. 67-77.
31. Brynjolfsson, Erik, Hitt, Lorin (1996). "Paradox lost? Firm-level Evidence on the Returns to Information Systems Spending", *Management Science*, April, Vol. 42, No. 4, pp. 541-558.
32. Parsons, D., Gotlieb, C.C. and Denny, M. (1993). "Productivity and Computers in Canadian Banking", Z. Griliches and J.Mairesse (Eds.), *Productivity Issues in Services at the Micro Level*, Kluwer, Boston.
33. Balasubramanya S., "IT wave breaks over banking", THE CITY, Aug – Sept 2002.
34. Rajashekhara, K.S. "Application of IT in Banking", Yojana, July 04.
35. Vij, Madhu "The New World of Banking: A Paradigm shift", Journal of Managemen, Research, Vol. 3, December 2003.
36. Gulati, V.P., Sivakumaran M.V., C. Manognaa "IT framework for Indian banking sector", ASCI Journal of Management 31 (1&2). 67-77 (2002).
37. Ananthakrishnan, G. "Customer Service in Banks", Vinimaya, Vol. XXV, No.3, 2004-05.
38. Rao Akula Rajgopal. "Sprightliness of Urban Cooperative Banks : A Study".
39. Morrison, C.J. and Berndt, E.R. (1990). "Assessing the Productivity of Information Technology Equipment in the U.S Manufacturing Industries", *National Bureau of Economic Research Working Paper* #3582, January.
40. Loveman, G.W. (1994). "*An Assessment of the Productivity Impact of Information Technologies*", T.J. Allen and M.S. Scott Morton (Eds.), Information Technology and the Corporation of the 1990s: Research Studies, MIT Press, Cambridge MA.
41. Lichtenberg, F. (1995). "The Output Contributions of Computer Equipment and Personnel: A Firm-Level Analysis," *Economics of Innovation and New Technology*, Vol. 3, p. 201-217.
42. Gulati, V. P. "Information Technology Application in Indian Banking: Better Late than Never!", "NewsLetter", Volume 6, No. 3, July 1996.
43. Mishra, A. K. (Prof. At IIM Lucknow). Internet Banking in India, The Maharashtra Cooperative Quarterly, http://www.banknetindia.com/ banking/ ibkg.htm.
44. Jadhav, A. S., Mrs. R. A. Jadhav. "Status of e-banking in India", National annual convention of CSI 2004.

45. Hebbar Raveendranath. "Building trust in E-Banking", Vinimaya, Vol. XXIV, No. 4, 2003-04.
46. V. Radha. "Preventing Technology Based Bank Frauds", "The Journal of Internet Banking and Commerce", Dec. 2008, Vol. 13, No. 3.
47. D. Joe Edwinraj, "Information Technology: The emerging driving force in cooperative banks", Cooperative Perspective: Vol. 40, No. 1, April–June 05.
48. Kamath, K V, Kohli, S S, Shenoy, P S, Ranjana Kumar, Nayak R M, and Kuppuswamy, PT, N Ravichandran, "Indian Banking Sector: Challenges and Opportunities", Vikalpa, Vol. 28, No. 3, Jul-Sept. 2003.
49. Kunkalienkar, Manoj. "IT in Banking 2003 (Special) Perspectives of CEO's: Banking Software Companies" (http://www.banknetindia. com/special/ itb8b.htm).
50. Mishra, Sudarshana. "BFSI", PCQUEST, August 2004.
51. Mittal, R. K. and Dhingra Sanjay. "Technology in banking sector: issues and challenges", Vinimay, Vol. XXVII, No. 4, 2006-07.
52. A Subbiah & S Jayakumar, "Customer service in commercial banks in India: a study with reference to core banking", Vinimay, Vol. XXIX, No.3, 2008-2009.
53. R. Thanikodi, "Central cooperative banks in India: Problems and Remedies", Cooperative Perspectives, Vol. 40, No. 3 Oct-Dec 05.
54. Uppal, R. K. and Kaur, Rimpi. "Indian banking moving towards a better tomorrow", Vinimay, Vol. XXIX, No. 3, 2008-09.
55. Bagchi, Amaresh. "Banking system and economy: Indian experience", Vinimay, Vol. XXVIII, No. 2, 2007-08.
56. Uppal, R. K. and Dhingra, Sanjay. "Technology in banking sector: Issues and challenges", Vinimay, Vol. XXVII, No. 4, 2006-07.
57. Srivastava, R. M. "Indian commercial banks on path towards competitive efficiency", Vinimay, Vol. XXVII, No. 3, 2006-07.
58. Srivastava, R. M. and Nigam, Divya, "Retail Banking in India: prospects and challenges", Vinimay, Vol. XXVII, No. 1, 2006-07.
59. Mehta, J. "Indian Banking in 2010", Vinimay, Vol. XXVIII, No. 3, 2007-08.
60. Uppal, R. K. "Customer Perception of E-Banking Services of Indian Banks: Some Survey Evidence", The ICFAI University Journal of Bank Management, Volume VII, Issue-1 (Feb. 2008), p. 63-78.
61. Kamakodi, N., M Basheer Ahmed Khan. "Customer Expectations and Service Level in E-Banking Era: An Empirical Study", The ICFAI University Journal of Bank Management, Volume VII, Issue 4 (Nov. 2008), p. 50-70.
62. S. Venkata Seshaiah & Vunyale Narender. "Factors Affecting Customers' Choice of Retail Banking", ICFAI University Journal of Bank Management, Vol. VI, issue 1 (March 2007), p. 34-46.

D

E